BAGS
IN THE
ATTIC

A Mother's Courageous Journey of Escaping Abuse
and Evoking the Will to Survive the Odds

JOAN T. RANDALL

BAGS IN THE ATTIC
Published by Purposely Created Publishing Group™
Copyright © 2020 Joan T. Randall
All rights reserved.

Unless otherwise indicated, scripture quotations are from the Holy Bible, King James Version. All rights reserved.

Printed in the United States of America

ISBN: 978-1-64484-160-0

Special discounts are available on bu lk quantity purchases by book clubs, associations and special interest groups. For details email: sales@publishyourgift.com or call (888) 949-6228. For information log on to www.PublishYourGift.com

This book is dedicated to the women who taught me true love. They gave me the power to persevere and the will to find the strength to survive. They are my gifts from God. Without them, I would not be here. They are the complete essence of who I am—so different but so much alike. To my head and my heart, my left and right ventricle, my greatest accomplishments: my daughters Kaydene A. Suragh-Caban and Shayana M. Oakley.

I love you both more than words can convey!

TABLE OF CONTENTS

FOREWORD

Rarely do we get a glimpse into the real world of a woman, a wife, a daughter, a mother, and a person who provides the reader a window into the reality of her life in such a vulnerable way. Joan does just this in her book. In this provocative work, Joan courageously recounts the story of how she grew up in her native Jamaica, overcame significant odds with her father and mother's relationship, faced the responsibility of helping to support her family financially, and gained the love she sought in relationships over the years. She further provides insight into a mother's journey with her children and how she ultimately fled a tumultuous situation of an abusive relationship to seek the freedom that was so richly deserved. Joan's tenacity is evident in her brave recount of how she was treated by Mr. and others drawn to abusive tactics in an effort to control her.

From the moment I met Joan, I knew something was different about her. I've never met a more confident, driven, brave, beautiful, and ostentatious woman such as Joan T. Randall. From the first conversation, where she engaged me with her amazing smile, warm embrace, and attentive eyes, her quiet confidence astounded me. She eased through the crowd with a sense of resilience that I did not quite comprehend until I understood her story even more. This work is truly a must-read for women around the world. Joan's resilience, boldness, bravery, and strength are testaments to how women everywhere can be when facing tribulations such as the ones she faced.

For women or men facing domestic violence and other forms of abuse, their voices are silenced by shame and embarrassment. No one knows how it feels to walk in their shoes except for those who have experienced this type of trauma. Joan slowly walks the reader through the emotional roller coaster of what it is like to endure these instances of ridicule, poor treatment, and confidence-stealing moments, providing solutions along the way. From how to recognize the signs of abuse to strategies she used to escape her abuser, Joan provides steps for every reader to take or share with others who need this information.

The agony a mother faces as she decides what's best for her children is unparalleled, and Joan brings this real emotional experience to the forefront of our lives through her book. As Joan was internally conflicted regarding the safety and well-being of her daughters, more so than her own, the readers can clearly see how selfless she was and how truly remarkable this story of overcoming adversity is. This book is unfortunately reminiscent of a common story held by many women across the world facing abuse and neglect. This work brings light to these sensitive issues and provides hope for all who seek answers for how they too can escape their situation.

To Joan and her brave daughters, thank you for sharing your story! You are saving so many.

Aimy S. L. Steele, PhD
North Carolina House of Representatives
Educator, Community Leader, and Advocate

PART I

UNFORTUNATE CIRCUMSTANCES

CHAPTER ONE

THE DARKEST DAY

I woke up fully intending to carry out my plan. I had thought it through over and over in my mind and even did a few practice runs. I knew this was it! I was unable to comprehend, think, or see another way out. I was dying inside. I had been silently screaming for help. If someone had just looked closer into my eyes or seen past the lies I told, they would have known that I was in trouble. They would have asked the right questions, and maybe—just maybe—I would have told them the truth. The truth was embarrassing. The truth hurt. The fact was, I did not want to live anymore. I wanted to end it. I wanted to go to sleep permanently, but—wait, there is that "but." My mind raced. I could not leave my girls alone. I could not leave them to the unknown. I was not sure what kind of life they would have if I left them. Would they be placed in a foster home? Would a family member get custody of them? Would they end up together or apart? I loved them too much to leave them in a world of uncertainty, the same one that I was residing in.

This was not how I had imagined my life when I boarded the plane to come to the United States. This type of living was not part of the plan. Why did I leave my home? Why did I leave Jamaica, my family, and my friends to come here to be treated this way? Why did I think he was my knight in shining armor? It was all a sham, a pretense. He was not who I thought he was. What was it about me that made him so mean and angry? Why now, when I had moved in with him and become his wife? What did I do to deserve this life and this treatment? I had a life filled with love back home. Yes, I knew I hurt Shawn. I did not tell him that I was leaving to come to the United States to be with another man. He only knew I was going, but I had left out the part about the man. I justified my dishonesty by thinking that Shawn was seeing someone else, so it was not going to work out anyway. Me leaving for the United States was what I thought was best for my baby girl and me. Even though I was still troubled and highly upset with my dad for how he publicly humiliated my mom, in Jamaica, I was surrounded by love. The love of family, great friends, my daughter, and Shawn. As I thought about Shawn, a wave of sadness swept over me, and I sobbed uncontrollably. My heart was broken. I left the guy I loved for what I thought would be a better life, and because of my dishonesty, I was being punished. I felt hopeless and shattered.

Now, here I was, with another justification. I was tired of the life I'd been living. I wanted to go to sleep, I needed to rest, and I wanted my girls to be with me. My pillow was soaked with tears from all the crying the night before. This had become the norm. I knew how to sob without making a sound. I would get severe chest pains and anxiety, but I'd rather suffer through that than let anyone know I was crying. Too often, I would cry when Mr. and I argued and he became aggressive. He would ask why I was crying, and that would be followed by "Why are you so stupid?," or "That is stupid," or "You are stupid." "Stupid" was one of his favorite words. So when I cried at night, if he happened to be in bed, which had become less frequent over the years, the tears were silent.

On this specific day, tears pouring down my face as I sat in bed alone in the silence and darkness of the wee hours of the morning, every emotion swept through my body. I felt empty, alone, lost, hopeless, scared, defeated, and depressed. I was thirty years old, and I felt like a failure. I had failed my daughters. The life I had brought them into was unfair for them. My sweet love Kay, my firstborn, was ushered into this life that was cold and unfamiliar. She did not deserve it. Thinking about her and what she had experienced since she came to live with us made my body feel as if it were going to break into pieces. I knew the transition for her to the States had been a very difficult one. I saw the distance and the sadness in her eyes every day. The burden in my heart was too heavy to carry. I wept until my eyes were almost swollen shut and my chest felt as if my heart had been taken out. I wrapped my arms around my stomach and squeezed as hard as I could, trying to fill the emptiness, but it was futile. I was a shell of a person. I had no money, and I was afraid to ask my family for help. I was too prideful to tell them I was being abused. I was embarrassed to tell my coworkers, and every friendship that I had established since I moved to New Jersey was somewhat dissolved because Mr. did not like me having friends. I was isolated in New Jersey, and there was no one to talk to.

No matter how I searched my heart and my mind, I could not find a shimmer of light or hope. The darkness of the cloud of abuse had wrapped me in chains that I was unable to break free from, and the only solace I felt was the release of knowing we were going to go to sleep forever, never to suffer from the pain of the world again.

This would go down easy, just like I'd practiced. I would go to Kay's room first, and while she lay sleeping, I would put one bullet to her head and put her to sleep permanently. She would never feel it. Then I'd go to Shay's room and do the same, and then to my bedroom for the final one in my head. We would finally be at rest, at peace, and we would sleep forever together. At that moment, the thought of sleep and being at peace gave me comfort. Looking back, I realize that I was such a broken vessel and that the thought of carrying out this action was so irrational. However, at that moment, I thought that I was doing the right thing, and we were just going to be at rest.

As I got up off the bed and walked to get the gun, my heart was pounding. I retrieved it from the closet. It was small with a pearl handle. I thought to myself that it would not really do too much damage if it was used while they slept. It would not hurt because they would not feel it. My face was wet from the tears, and my heart was heavy. It was pre-dawn, and Mr. was not home. It had become customary for him to come back right before dawn and sleep in the family room downstairs. I thought about him coming home and not knowing we were dead. He would eventually find us, and I quickly dismissed from my mind the thought of what he would do or how he would react. After all, I did not care anymore. I wanted to hurt him as much as he had hurt me physically, verbally, and emotionally.

My eyes adjusted to the dimly lit room and closet. I was afraid to turn on the lights for fear of seeing my reflection in the mirror or a glimpse of my shadow that may give me second thoughts about what I was going to do. As I walked out of the closet and back to the bedroom, I saw the softness of the dawn peeking its head through my bedroom window. I stopped and stared at its beauty for a moment and thought what a beautiful morning it was to go home to God. I closed my eyes for a few seconds and got lost in the serenity and peace I suddenly felt. I took a deep breath in and exhaled but was startled by the sound of someone opening the bedroom door. I froze.

Right away, I thought it was Mr., but I had not heard the garage door open, so it could not be him. It was too early for the girls to be up, so who would be opening the bedroom door? A cold sweat, accompanied by waves of nervousness and anxiety, washed over me. Not now, no! I had been planning this for too long. I did not have a plan B, and I was not sure I would dare to do it again if I was interrupted. I remained still, staring at the dawn. I was shaking like a leaf, afraid to move. The gun was in my hand, and my mind was racing. What do I do? It was as if my feet were too heavy to move. As hard as I tried, I could not pick up my feet. The door slowly opened, and my heart sank as I heard a tiny little whisper.

"Mommy?"

Oh, God no, I thought. There, in the dim light of the dawn, with arms outstretched feeling her way around the room, was my three-and-a-half-year-old baby girl, Shay.

"Mommy, Mommy, where are you?"

She reached the side of the bed that I slept in and felt around for my body. It was customary for her to wake up and come crawl in bed with me, but she never woke this early. I did not want to startle her, so I softly said, "I am right here, baby."

That's when she turned and saw me. She ran over to me and wrapped her arms around my legs. I could not do anything; there was no way that I could carry out my plan while she was awake. I did not have the heart for that. I quickly placed my right hand holding the gun behind my back and used my left hand to pull her closer to my body. I slowly sat on the floor with my legs crossed and secretly placed the gun under my right thigh, out of her sight. I pulled her little body into my arms and hugged her. She laid her head on my shoulder.

The tears rushed out of me in a torrential downpour, but I did not make a sound—what I was used to. Oh, God, I thought, I can't do this. Not here, not now, why, why, why? Everything got messed up and there was no plan B. What was next? Here I was, sitting on the floor with my arms around my baby's body, a broken mother, empty, tired, with no strength left to fight, to fight with Mr. or to go on. I thought that God had abandoned me, abandoned us. I had called on Him so many times, and He was not there. Why did He turn his back on my babies and me? I was a great person: kind, loving, and caring. I had a compassionate heart. Why would God bring me here and leave me in this mess? I wrote so many letters to Him in my journal, but He did not answer any of them. As the tears and emotions poured from me for what seemed like forever but was only a few minutes, my baby lifted her head from my shoulder and placed both of her hands on my face. The sky had begun to clear, and the first rays of the morning were creeping through the windows. She could see my face plainly. She looked into my eyes, seeing that they were swollen and my face wet. With both of her hands still on my face and with the most angelic and innocent voice, she asked me, "Mommy, are you sad?"

I was taken aback by the question, but I mustered up the strength in a strained, shaken voice to say, "Yes, Mommy is sad."

What she told me next changed my life forever. She said, "Don't worry, Mommy, I can give you strength."

"How would you do that?" I asked her.

She placed both of her hands around my neck, squeezed with all the strength she could find in her three-and-a-half-year-old body, and said, "Here is the strength, Mommy. I am giving you my strength."

She held me so tight, as if she was holding on for her life. Almost immediately, through her hug, I felt energy pass from her body into mine. I looked at the window and noticed the sunlight was coming through and hitting her back. That energy was passing through her body and into my mine. I felt a strange stirring, a renewing that caught my soul, and I felt my eyes open. Somehow, I was awakened. I woke out of what seemed like a long sleep. I had not felt this type of clarity in years. Something happened.

I held on to my baby so tightly and cried out to God, "Thank you, thank you, thank you, God."

I sobbed out loud.

She patted my back as she said, "It's going to be okay, Mommy, it's going to be okay."

The baby consoled her mother.

The fog that I had lived in for years was gone. I knew that I could never take their lives or mine. God showed me His love by using my daughter to get my attention. Little did Shay know that she saved our lives that day. I recognize now that God was always there. I just could not see Him through the clouds, the haze of domestic abuse, the life of confusion. How did I get here? As I reflected on the decision that I had made, to take my life and the lives of my children, I could not help but think back to the series of events that led to that moment.

CHAPTER TWO

ACQUIESCING

I had amazing parents. I grew up seeing unconditional love between my mom and dad. My mom was the stern disciplinarian, and Dad was the laid-back cool guy. Dad was my idol. He could never do anything wrong in my eyes. I loved him more than love itself. He told me that when I was a baby, I was crying so hard one night until I stopped breathing and my body started turning blue. My mom was crying when she noticed I was unresponsive, and Dad got scared. This was in the sixties in Jamaica, so getting a ride to go to a hospital would have taken hours, if it was even possible to get there. My quick-thinking father picked up my lifeless body, stood on a chair, and held my body as close as he could under the light bulb in the ceiling. He told me that he cried out to God in prayer and shook me gently as the heat from the bulb penetrated my stomach. As he continued to pray, I coughed and started crying again. They were both relieved. He always told me that he had saved my life, and maybe that's why I loved him so much.

I was the oldest of three from the union of my mom and dad. I also had older half-brothers and a sister. I was born in the capital of Jamaica, Kingston, and as a family, we lived a pretty good life. My dad worked as a waiter, and my mom stayed at home and took care of us. I loved our home in the city. When I was about to start high school, my dad convinced my mom to pack up and move to a rural area in the country, so he could help his sister, my aunt, take care of their aging and ailing father who had gone blind. It was hard for my aunt to shoulder the full responsibility of my grandfather, so my dad being there to assist in that process would be helpful to her. My dad loved his sister, and after months of convincing, my mom acquiesced.

I used to love going to the country to visit my grandparents because it was always an adventure. But I did not want to live there permanently. This move completely changed our lives in several ways, and I sometimes wondered how different my life would have been if we had not made that move. I wanted to go to the high school in the city that I had chosen. I worked hard to pass my exams to get into that school. I used to ride by on the bus and daydream about wearing the uniform of Holy Childhood High. I loved the sophisticated wardrobe with the blue pleated skirt, white blouse, and blue necktie. I was sad that I had to transfer to the school in the country, though it turned out to be a fantastic school, and I am a proud alum of Titchfield High School in Port Antonio, Portland.

We lived in a few different places in the country until we finally settled in at my grandparents' home. My aunt and her children lived there as well. Things were tough. There was no electricity or indoor toilet—things we were accustomed to. The kitchen was small.

We had a kerosene oil stove, but most of the time, Mom had to cook outside on a wood fire.

Our family of five lived in two rooms. The house was in a less-than-good condition. I felt embarrassed getting off the bus at the house because its outer physical state. The white wall that made up the veranda in front of the house had ugly mildew, and my grandmother's tomb sat on one side of the yard. I would get off at the bus stop before or after my home and then walk back. Many days, I went to school without lunch or lunch money, but I always managed to get something to eat. A friend would share their lunch with me, or someone would buy me lunch. During my senior year of high school, I had to go to a neighbor's house to study because the constant straining of my eyes to study by the glow of a kerosene lamp had started to affect my vision. My neighbor was gracious enough to allow me to study in his home so I could use the electric lights.

My mother had made the ultimate sacrifice. She loved my dad so much and was willing to give up the life she knew, the life she was comfortable with, for one that was uncertain. As a stay-at-home mom, she inadvertently became the full-time caretaker for my blind grandfather because my dad and aunt had full-time jobs. But she never complained. She kept her calm even when my grandfather called her names and spoke out of character. She recognized that he had started to develop early signs of dementia, so she ignored his insults. Sometimes the way my grandfather treated my mom made me sad and angry. I knew it had to hurt my mom deeply, but she was such a woman of strength and character that she took it without verbalizing her pain. Fortunately, my mom and my aunt were best friends and spent a lot of time together. They loved each other. And since we shared the home with my aunt and my cousins, we became one big family filled with love, and that overrode the material lack.

My siblings and I adjusted to the change in lifestyle, but there was still a yearning in me to be different from what I saw around me. I would sit and daydream about life beyond Jamaica, imagining myself on a stage, talking to hundreds of people, reading the news, or having power and influence. I never understood where that came from. I was different from my siblings and cousins. While they played, I sat and watched them, but I was never truly present. I was always in a different world, daydreaming, writing, or listening to music. I had an affinity for learning and I excelled in school. I wondered what life was like beyond the horizon. Even as a teenager, I felt like Jamaica was a box—and I never liked boxes.

When I was fourteen years old, I met a handsome guy named Tony, who told me he was eighteen. We developed a relationship, and he was my escape. He took me out on his motorcycle, and we had a lot of fun. I knew I was way too young for that type of relationship, but no one stopped me from seeing him. I found out, after two years of being in a relationship with him, that he was actually ten years older than me. But at that time, it didn't really matter. I was so in love with Tony, and spending time with him made me happy. Once I started dating him, I always had money for lunch.

When I graduated high school, I was accepted into Church Teachers' College. I was so excited. I wanted to leave home and experience living in a college dorm with dorm mates. I knew there would be electricity, a washing machine, and a refrigerator—things we did not have in our country home. After I went to my college orientation, I was excited to move away—but all that came to a halt when my dad told me that I needed to put college on hold and get a job to help him take care of my younger brother and sister. I was very disappointed that my dad didn't see the value in college as much as my mother did. He thought that after high school, he had done enough to take care of me, and now it was my time to help myself and him. In hindsight, I realize he had come from a generation of lack—that's the only thing he saw around him, and that was the culture—so it was natural for him to expect the same of me. My mother was different. She wanted the best for her children and was proud that I had gotten into college. If it were left up to her, solely, I would have gone straight to college after high school. But, yet again, she gave in to my father's wishes.

On the one hand, I was devastated, but the thought of working and making my own money intrigued me. I decided to postpone college for a year so I could help the family financially. I was fortunate enough to get a job right after I gave up going away to college. I secured full-time employment as an accounts receivable clerk with an electric company. I was thrilled to get this coveted job. People who were more qualified than I was applied for the position, but the offer was made to me. It just so happened that the district manager of this office was the father of a classmate and friend. I was astounded at the financial offer I received to work for this company. Straight out of high school, I had landed a job paying me almost triple the average salary at that time. I was going to be making big bucks, and boy, was I happy.

After orientation and training, I settled into working full time. I absolutely loved it. My first assignment was to collect electric bill payments. I worked my way up and started to travel to other neighboring towns and cities to work in various capacities. The company provided room and board for those assignments outside of my typical commute. Within the first year of working with the electric company, I asked the technicians to come to my home and wire it for electricity. That was such a big deal. I felt so accomplished and happy that I was able to make this happen for my family. I finally did it, I thought. After so many years without electricity, we finally had it in our home.

Though things were going well for my career, I started to feel uncomfortable around the district manager. He had become extremely friendly with me and overly touchy-feely. I shrugged it off as him being caring in a fatherly way, but his actions got more and more inappropriate. Then the unthinkable happened. He called me into his office one day and asked me to close the door behind me. Immediately, my heart started pounding! I could hear the beating in my ears. I felt all my internal organs shaking. Did I do something wrong? Was I in trouble? If so, why would he not have my immediate supervisor in the office with me if there was an issue?

That was when I realized that all he wanted was full access to me without interruption. Closing the door was his way of having me all to himself. What he said next almost made me wish I was in trouble instead. He called me over to him and told me to sit on his lap. I was stunned. I pretended I did not hear his command and said, "Excuse me?"

"Come and sit on my lap," he repeated. "I am not going to hurt you."

I obeyed. I walked over to him and sat on his lap, and he proceeded to unbutton my blouse. He placed his hand under my bra and started massaging my breasts. It was as if time stood still. I sat there, frozen in disbelief. When he had his share of excitement, he kissed me on the cheek, redid the buttons of my blouse, and told me I could go back to work. I felt dirty and violated. I kept swallowing hard to fight the tears back.

I put on my signature smile as I opened the door and walked out of his office.

I knew I would never be able to tell anyone. I was helping to support my family. I loved my job and I would never want to lose it. No one ever left this company. They spent their whole lives there because of the fantastic benefits and perks the job provided. Even if I told someone, they would never believe me. He was too influential in the town. I wondered if he was doing the same thing to the other female employees. I never told anyone, and it continued to happen on and off for a couple of years until he finally left the company and a new district manager took over.

My relationship continued with my long-time love, Tony, and six years later, at twenty years old, I gave birth to my beautiful firstborn daughter, Kay. I had every intention of going back to school at a later date, but at that point, I knew that pursuing higher education was no longer possible. I had become a mother. I accepted that outcome, and my daughter became my priority. What I did not know was that betrayal was about to destroy my family as I knew it.

CHAPTER THREE

THE BETRAYAL

I always knew my father was a flirt. I had seen him flirt with tons of women, but I never thought it went beyond that. One day, I went to surprise him at his job and found a very young woman in his workshop with him. I was distraught, and he told her to leave. He asked me not to mention it to my mom, and I kept it our secret.

I had a beautiful necklace that was sent to me as a gift from my pen pal, Mary, who lived in Greece. This necklace was one of a kind. It went missing, and I cried for days. One day, I took the bus into town, and I saw a woman in my necklace. I felt like my heart stopped because the woman wearing my necklace was the same young woman I had caught my dad with months earlier. I wanted to say something to her, but I felt numb. My heart was pounding as the tears streamed down my cheeks on the bus. My dad had obviously taken my necklace without my knowledge and given it to this woman. I was so hurt. My throat felt swollen. I felt as if I were losing air in my lungs. I realized that there was more to my dad and this woman. I was already keeping the secret from my mom, and now this? At that moment, I became angry. How could he do this to me? What is he doing to his family?. I later asked my dad about the necklace, telling him I saw the woman wearing it on the bus. He told me that she must have stolen it. I knew he was lying. I never saw my necklace—or that woman—again.

Around the same time as the necklace incident, I started noticing changes in my parent's relationship. Dad was coming home later and later. When Mom asked about his whereabouts, he made up excuses. There was tension between them—a type of stress I had never seen in all the years I knew my parents. My mother became extremely sad. I would sometimes hear her cry at night.

Then the rumors started about my dad seeing another woman who lived down the street from our home. I started putting it all together. He was not coming home until the wee hours of the morning, and the gossip circulating within the small town we resided in made it clear that my dad was seeing someone else. Six months later, all my fears came true. He came home, took all his clothes, and left. He moved out, leaving my mother for a woman who lived less than a half-mile from our home and was only a few years older than myself. He betrayed the woman who trusted him with everything that she had.

My mother fulfilled the role of a full-time caretaker for my grandfather until he passed away. My father had promised us that when granddad died, he would build a house for us on the property that was left for him, and we would no longer have to live in the main house with the rest of the family. My mom's desire was for us to have our own home. However, that promise was broken, and Dad made absolutely no effort to build a house for us. He later sold the property he had inherited to his brother, my uncle, to marry his mistress and renovate her home. He abandoned my mom and betrayed his children. It was a devastating blow to me, the child he saved, the child who loved him more than love.

I don't think my mother ever got over the pain of my dad's broken promise. Mom trusted him to take care of her and her children because we were all she had. She sacrificed who she was for us. She went without, so we could have. She put herself last, so we could be first. She loved my dad with every fiber of her being, more than she loved herself. She treated my father like a king, and he left her. He left us. There were days when my mom would sit on the veranda, and she would see my dad walk by our home with his then mistress. She saw them together all the time. He did not care that he broke her heart, and ours, into one million pieces.

I was hurt and heartbroken for my mom. I decided I was going to ask my dad what he was thinking. Why was he doing this to us? One day, my dad and I had a heated discussion. I told him I was going to talk to this woman about her destroying our family. He got so angry with me that for the first time in my life, my father pointed his finger in my face and used profanity to threaten me. My heart stopped beating for a second. Who was this man? I did not recognize him as my dad.

He had changed so much. What did this lady do to him for him to abandon his wife of over twenty years and his children?

A few months later, we got the most devastating news. His mistress was pregnant! I was broken, I was hurt, I cried for my mother. He betrayed her in the worst way ever, in front of an entire community of people. He took her from her home in Kingston and brought her miles away to the country, apart from the people she knew, from a life she knew, and then he turned his back on her. If one child was not bad enough, he fathered a second child with his mistress a few years later. He committed the ultimate betrayal.

When I found out about the first child he fathered with his mistress, I made a decision to move out of the family home. There was no reason to stay now that he was building another family. In my heart, I was hoping that he and mom would reconcile, but I knew that having a child while still married to my mom was the nail in the coffin. Now that a child was in the picture, he was permanently gone. I had a great job, and I could afford to start my own life with my daughter, but I also wanted my mother out of that little town so she could get her dignity back. I relocated to the capital, and I took my mother, my younger sister Shelly, and my daughter Kay away from the shame and embarrassment of my father's betrayal. With my mom, my sister, and my daughter safely out of the little Snow Hill town, I was happy. Mom, although hurting, never complained. She hid the pain she was feeling from us.

The experience with my father changed me. I felt like my heart turned cold and hard, and I did not trust men. After seven years with my boyfriend, Tony, the father of my daughter, I walked away from the relationship. I wanted more out of life, and I did not think he could give it to me. He did not like change, and I needed change. I was ambitious. I wanted more than average for my daughter, and he was content on living an average life. There is nothing wrong with that, but I was evolving. I had never bought into the generational expectation of the lack mentality. I knew there was an entire world out there filled with abundance, and I wanted that. I wanted to explore the world outside of Jamaica. I was itching for more, and in some strange way, that desire to be different created a shift in my mind. I felt as if I had outgrown my daughter's father.

I got involved in other relationships, but I was never genuinely faithful to any of the men. I had promised myself that I would never let any man betray me the way my dad had. At one point, I was simultaneously dating three men who resided in different parts of Jamaica. They each satisfied a need I was searching for. They all took care of me financially, and for some strange reason, it made me feel powerful. I had one-night stands as a choice. It never phased me because I was in total control of who I wanted and when I wanted them, and they were never strong enough to tell me no.

Then there were the sugar daddies. They were older—old enough to be my father. As a matter of fact, two of them had daughters who were my age and older. I did not realize that I was repeating the behaviors of my dad because I was so hurt. I was involuntarily self-destructing without a clue. Unfortunately, the taboo of mature men yearning for girls young enough to be their daughters was a norm in our society. These men craved the innocence of my youth and lusted after the hot spring of my curvy, voluptuous body. They offered me shiny things: jewelry, clothes, shoes, and money. I willingly quenched their thirst and took all they gave me and then some. And because they worked in different areas of the island, it was easy to slip away and engage with them separately. B was my favorite. He was short in stature and full of personality. His energy was infectious. Anyone that came in contact with him was drawn to his big, genuine smile. He loved my mother and would always make time to see her and give her gifts.

These men were paying my bills, so I had money to do whatever, and I was in control of my lifestyle. But I was never satisfied. I was not truly happy. I pretended to be okay around everyone as I struggled with the breakdown of my parents' relationship and the gaping hole left in my heart by my dad.

One day, it all caught up with me. One of the three men, with whom I had the more serious relationship, found out I was cheating. He was hurt, and we broke up, but it never affected me emotionally. One of the other guys also found out about my promiscuous actions and tried to hurt me. He pulled a knife on me during a heated conversation and told me he was going to stab me to death. I screamed for help, and someone heard and came to my rescue. They called the cops, and he was arrested. I did not press charges, so they had to release him from lockup. I dissolved the relationship and walked away from that nightmare.

I knew then that I was playing Russian Roulette with my life because of my internalized pain, so I slowed it down. I made the decision to stop the craziness. I knew I was unavailable for a genuine intimate commitment, but I still wanted comfort and to satisfy the almost unquenchable physical desires that raged in my body.

Then I met Shawn. He was doing contract work with the electric company I worked for, and he would travel from his hometown of Kingston to Port Antonio on Monday mornings and leave on Friday evenings to go back home. We started spending a lot of time together. He was kind and gentle with an attractively shy smile. He was about 6'1" and athletically built with smooth caramel skin. I loved the way his bow legs looked in his jeans. He spoke with a lisp and would lick his lips like LL Cool J. His eyes were inviting, and he exuded confidence. He was a beautiful specimen of a man, and we were instantly attracted to each other.

Our chemistry was electric, and soon we became inseparable, spending every evening of the work week together at my home. With him, I would laugh all day.

With him, I was able let my guard down. He made me feel love again. His name for me was "my girl" and I loved it because it made me feel super special. He told me about his lady back home, and I was okay with it. She was all the way on the other side of the island, and I wanted to enjoy what we had while it lasted. I was his girl away from home. We dated for almost two years, and I loved every minute of it. When Shawn and I made love, it felt like the earth stopped moving. He took me on a journey of intimacy that was unique, different, and exciting. It was my first time experiencing that depth. I loved him.

Our love grew internally, and soon, a visible bump started to show. I did not know what to do. The morning sickness was awful. Neither of us were ready for another baby. My little girl was three, and Shawn had a daughter with his lady back home. After much discussion, tears, and contemplation, we made the decision to do what was best for everyone involved. I had an abortion. Afterward, we were much more careful about using protection, so it would not happen again. There came a point in the relationship when I wanted much more from Shawn than he could give or commit to, and it put a strain on our union—and then a new man came into my life unexpectedly and changed everything.

CHAPTER FOUR

MR.

A car pulled up beside me as I was walking home from work. The driver with dreads and an accent asked me for directions, and my interest was peaked. He had the most amazing teeth and smile. I gave him the instructions to where he wanted to go, and he offered me a ride home. I refused, telling him I was only a few blocks away from home. He was not taking no for an answer, and I was not getting into the car with him. I continued to walk as he drove beside me, giving me compliments and asking questions. When he asked me if I had a boyfriend, I immediately said no. It was accurate in some sense because Shawn had a lady, but it was also a lie because Shawn was in my life. It was a truth-lie! I justified it in my mind knowing the current situation with Shawn.

This guy drove his car beside me the whole way home. Once there, he stopped and got out to talk to me. We had a long conversation about a variety of things, and it was lovely. He had a great, refreshing sense of humor. I found out he was on vacation from the United States, and he was visiting his family in town. He asked if he could take me out that evening. I declined but agreed to go out with him over the weekend.

I enjoyed our date. I had a ton of fun learning about this new guy. One thing led to another, and another, and another, and the next thing I knew, I was in a whirlwind romance with him. His name was Mr. I am not sure if it was the Jamaican-American accent that got to me or the opportunities that came swirling around in my head that made me believe everything he told me. This could be my chance, I thought. This may just be my ticket out of Jamaica.

Mr. was about 5'11" and slim built. He was very charming, and his laugh would make anyone laugh. It came from his soul. He was well-groomed and impeccably dressed. Everything he used on his body— soap, moisturizer, fragrance—was made from essential oils. His mysterious presence enamored me. His eyes were dark, and I somehow sensed that it held a lot of secrets. Things moved fast.

Shortly after we met, he went back to the United States, but we kept in touch daily. The conversations quickly deepened, and we expressed our love for each other. He was a Rastafarian who revered the exiled Ethiopian Emperor, Haile Selassie. When he found out that Emperor Selassie and I shared the same birthdate, July 23, he was convinced he had found his queen. I felt like royalty knowing that I shared the same birthday with the Emperor. He told me he had to have me. In my naivety, I thought he was the one.

After five months of this long-distance intensity, he was ready for me to relocate to the United States to be with him and become his wife. He was charismatic and convincing. I bought into everything he said, hook, line, and, sinker. He threw out the net, and I was the catch. Then he reeled me in, and I was his dinner.

My goodness, was this really happening? Was this a sign that I was finally getting the chance to leave Jamaica? To go across the horizon to the place I dreamt about for years? I was excited and scared at the same time. Did I know enough about him to give up my life as I knew it to travel to the United States? To convince me that he was the real deal, he connected me to his family who lived in the same town. It turned out that I knew his aunt and cousin really well, which gave me a level of comfort.

Meanwhile, Shawn's contract work with the electric company was getting less frequent, so he was not traveling as often to my city. I was so preoccupied with Mr. that I was not upset about not seeing Shawn as much. I was torn and a little confused by my situation because I had a deep, genuine love for Shawn, but I was now on a different level, and no one was going to stop this ship from sailing. I had bought into this new relationship with Mr. so much that I refused to acknowledge the little signs that were peeking their heads out at me.

When I told my mom I was going to take a chance and relocate to the United States, she begged me to rethink my decision. She asked me several times if I truly knew him, but I did not want to hear anything from anyone who could have swayed my mind or placed doubt in my heart. I was determined to go. I was not letting this opportunity pass me by. Furthermore, I knew his aunt and his cousin, and they always said great things about him, so that was that.

I happily resigned from my seven-year career with the electric company only six months after I met Mr. I began preparing for my new life in the United States. The plan was to leave my baby with my mom until I was settled, and then I would take her up to the States. Leaving Jamaica was bittersweet. The sweet part was going to be with Mr. and having countless opportunities to spread my wings in a new land—the land of opportunities as I came to know it. The bitter part was leaving my beautiful baby girl, Kay, behind. Although I knew she would be in good hands with my mother and my sister, it ripped at my heart. I was also sad that I was leaving Shawn. He was very special to me, and he came into my life at a time when I needed a calming force. He showed me love, tenderness, and comfort. When I told him I was leaving, I did not tell him the whole truth. I did not want him to know that I was leaving to go be with another man. I am not sure why I lied. I was torn between them. Even though I knew that Shawn had a lady, I could not turn off the real love I had for him. Not too long after I left Jamaica, he and his lady broke up.

I cried the day I was going to the airport. I was about to tread in unknown waters. I was leaving the only life I had known, and I did not know what the future held for me. The one thing that kept me going was knowing that the reason I was doing this was to create the foundation of a better life for my daughter. This was for her as much as it was for me. We were a package deal, and Mr. knew that and accepted it. We agreed that as soon as I got settled, she would make the trip to be with us.

I knew I was going to miss my mom, my rock. She had slowly started her own healing process and was on speaking terms with my dad even though he was still living with his mistress and their two young children. I was sort of happy that I was leaving the situation with my dad behind me, but though his betrayal truly affected me emotionally, my love for him was still there.

I was ready to say goodbye to Jamaica. I had outgrown it all. There were butterflies in my stomach every time I thought about Mr., and I pictured a beautiful life with my knight in shining armor. I told myself that I loved him, but deep down, I was not sure of that. However, I knew that I could grow to love him. After all, he was making my dream come true—my dream of leaving the box. I wanted more significance, I wanted better, I wanted more, and I wanted to see the world through a new set of lenses. I needed to experience life beyond the horizon. The one I would sit and stare at every day as a teenager on the verandah of my grandfather's home or under a tree. In that magical scene, the blue sky met the Caribbean Ocean.

I had always wondered what kind of world lay beyond it. After years of wondering, the opportunity was now a reality. The butterflies I was feeling were expected, I told myself, but way deep down in the pit of my stomach, I was scared. Did I truly know this man?

CHAPTER FIVE

A DREAM REALIZED

Mr. was waiting for us when we landed in Texas. His cousin had made the trip with me because it was my first time traveling to the United States. I was happy that I did not have to go alone. We met in Texas because Mr. had a business meeting, after which we would drive to Philadelphia where I would make my new home with him.

When I arrived in the States, the air felt different. Even the smell was unique. It was late spring, and the temperature was cool. Philadelphia was the City of Brotherly Love, and my new home was on Bainbridge Street. I was mesmerized by the high-rise buildings in the town and the close proximity to everything. Pharmacies, restaurants, retail shops, banks, and movie theaters were all in walking distance.

I met Mr.'s daughter, Dami, who was eleven. My daughter was four, so I was unsure of how to parent a preteen, but I was willing to try. It was a little awkward at first, but eventually, we bonded. Dami was shy but sweet, and as we spent more time together, she opened up, becoming more like a little sister to me than a daughter. There was always a sadness in her eyes, and I quickly observed that her dad was cold and stern toward her. When he addressed her, his tone was strict, and I can't recall him ever hugging her or telling her he loved her. So I gave her all the love I had in my heart.

Mr. also had two sons, who were one and two years younger than Dami, but he was never in their lives the way a father should be. The younger of the two boys got into a lot of trouble at school for misbehaving, and their mother kept trying to get Mr. to be more present in their lives. But I felt like he just never cared.

I saw a change in Mr. almost immediately after I moved in. He appeared more agitated than I could remember, and within the first few weeks of me moving in with him, it started. I went out without telling him, and he got angry, saying that life in the United States is dangerous. I tried to explain to him that I needed some toiletries, and the pharmacy was just across the street, so it wasn't a big deal. Without warning, he slapped me across my face for responding to him in what he called a disrespectful tone. I was shocked and started crying.

"Why did you hit me?" I asked.

"Shut up," he said.

The look in his eyes was chilling, and it was the first time I noticed that he had a lazy eye. It made him look sinister. I did not recognize who was standing before me. He was a different person from the guy I'd met in Jamaica. This was not the guy who had told me I was a queen and that he needed me.

When he calmed down, he apologized and told me that he wanted to make sure that I was safe and aware of the possible dangers around me. He promised he would never hit me again, and I believed him.

A few weeks later, I fell ill and went to the doctor, only to find out that I was pregnant. Mr. was ecstatic, but I felt confused. I found myself in a strange place emotionally, and I was trying to adjust to this new life. I knew I was not ready for a baby. I already had a daughter, and she was still in Jamaica. I missed her so much. I was not prepared for another child. I had plans to work on getting my daughter to move here, and a baby would put a pause on that plan. And from what I had seen from Mr. lately, I was uncertain that this is what I wanted. I felt helpless and nervous about telling him that I was not ready for a baby, so I kept those feelings to myself.

I spent most of my days with Dami. Mr. traveled to Texas a lot and for days at a time. He was gone all the time, and when he was around, he was at the health food retail store that he owned. He had a split personality. There were times when he was kind, caring, and funny, and there were times when he would not speak to me. He had terrible mood swings, and I was not sure how to act around him at times. Both Dami and I walked around the house on eggshells trying not to rock the boat, and it was exhausting.

There were days when I sobbed out of control because I felt so empty. I missed my family, and I missed Shawn. I felt guilty that I had lied to him about the reasons why I left Jamaica. But most of all, my heart ached for my baby girl. I felt as if there was a hole in my heart that only she could fill. I cried for Kay every day. My intentions for coming to the States were to provide a better life for her—for us. But now, I thought I might have made a mistake. Why did I leave the comfort of my home, my country, my parents, my beautiful baby girl, my friends, to be here in this cold and unfriendly house? Who is this guy that I gave up everything to be with? Why did I not listen to my mom when she said she was worried because I did not know him?

I called my mom and daughter in Jamaica as often as I could. The phone bill got ridiculously high, which upset Mr. He screamed and shouted at me to not make so many calls. Because I was not working, I had to rely on his money for everything. I had no choice but to cut back from calling Jamaica from the house phone. When I got money from him, I would buy a phone card and make the calls that way. Every time I called and spoke to my daughter, it was as if my soul was fed, giving me nourishment that would last me until I called again. But as soon as I hung up the phone, I would sob. Being away from my princess was killing me. The guilt of leaving her would haunt me for years to come.

Six weeks later, I had a miscarriage, for which Mr. blamed me somehow. He was despondent, and he cried, but deep down, I knew I wasn't ready for a baby, and I was still uncertain about what my future held. I had seen a different side of him—one I did not like. One that scared me. I went to see the doctor who confirmed my miscarriage and gave me a dilation and curettage procedure (D&C) to make sure that no abnormal tissues were left in the uterus. Mr. asked why it happened, and the doctor told him that a myriad of reasons could have caused it. I was adjusting to a new country, I was overly emotional, and worry and stress could have played a role in me losing the baby.

When we left the doctor's office, Mr. was empathetic toward me, which was sweet. Every so often, I saw glimpses of the loving guy I met back home. He was still in there, but I knew that he was shouldering all the responsibilities and that was a lot, so I would try not to do anything to make him upset. I knew that the constant crying over my daughter and the emptiness I felt from missing my family played a role in the miscarriage. And I was happy it happened that way.

CHAPTER SIX

AN UNLIKELY FRIEND

I occasionally worked at the health food grocery store Mr. owned. It was always great to get out of the house. When he was at the store, he was a different person. For some reason, the store environment made him calm. Maybe it was because he was dealing with customers. Whenever he was in that mood, I was happy and tried my best not to provoke him in any way.

There was a young woman who frequented the store, and I started to suspect that they were having an affair. One day after seeing them interact, I asked what was going on between them. He got so enraged and started screaming at me—all while we were in the store. This was a first. I was angry so I shouted back. We had a massive fight, in the store, in front of customers. He was calling me names and cursing at me for accusing him, and I was crying my eyes out. I could always trust my instinct, and I knew I was right.

A young man who I recognized as an employee from the pharmacy next door walked in and observed this crazy situation. He saw and heard the verbal abuse and how angry and furious Mr. was. Later that day, when I went to the pharmacy to get some medicine for my headache from all the crying, the young man who had been in the store earlier assisted me and was very kind. He whispered to me that I should not have to take that type of abuse and that I was beautiful and deserved better. His words brought more tears to my eyes. This was the first time I had heard the word "abuse" used in relation to any of my relationships and most certainly in regard to the one I had with Mr. I could not find the words to respond because I was so embarrassed. The man gave me his business card and told me I could call him anytime if I needed someone to talk to. His name was Richard, and he calmed me down, offering me his friendship.

During Mr.'s trips to Texas, Richard and I developed a great friendship. I was happy that I had found one friend who I could trust. I told him how I wanted to go back to school, and he suggested a school for me to get my GED. I had sent for my transcripts from my high school in Jamaica, but it was taking forever, so I enrolled in the school Richard suggested, successfully completed the GED courses, and earned my certificate. I felt better about having that piece of paper. Now I could enroll in college or get a job. Mr. knew I was in school but never showed that he cared one way or the other. I cannot recall him ever telling me congratulations.

One day, I left the store early because I was feeling so sad and overwhelmed. I told Mr. I had a headache and was going to take the bus home. Two stops before my house was Penn's Landing, a fantastic waterfront location overlooking the Delaware River. I decided to get off the bus at that stop. I felt the need to sit in silence and enjoy the stillness of the water. I wanted to be alone with my thoughts, and looking at the ocean and the horizon comforted me. The peace and serenity of the water allowed my mind to drift back to Jamaica. I thought of the days when I used to daydream that I was successful. But the harsh reality hit me. I had found out what was on the other side of the horizon, and up to this point, it was not what I had expected.

After spending some time sitting in peace and solace, I got on the bus and went home. It was early evening, and the sun was still in the sky. Mr. had left work early because he kept calling the house phone and I did not pick up. So he closed the store, came home, and was there waiting for me when I opened the door. As soon as I entered, a barrage of curse words greeted me. His eyes were red, and I thought I saw fire coming from his nostrils. He asked me where I had been. I tried to explain that I had stopped by Penn's Landing just to enjoy the water and to be at peace for a little while. That explanation was not good enough for him. He got so furious that he picked up a glass vase and threw it at me. I jumped out of the way, the vase hitting the wall and shattering into pieces. I feared for my life. I knew the next thing coming would be him beating on me. He had told me he would never hit me again after the first time he slapped me, but I was not confident that he would be able to control himself in this situation. I cried and screamed so loud and begged him not to hit me.

The neighbors could hear us. I was close enough to the front door to hear them outside saying, "they are fighting." I sat down on the floor and sobbed and told him repeatedly that I was sorry, and I would never do it again. I stopped talking and just listened as he threatened me with what he would do if I ever did something like that again. I was shaking like a wet kitten, and my heart was pounding in my ears. He verbally abused me for what seemed like hours, calling me names and cursing until he was tired, and then he left the house. After I gathered myself and thanked God for protecting me from that vase, I got up and swept up the fragments. On this particular day, Dami was visiting her aunt. She was not at home to experience the chaos, and I was happy about that. I took a shower and sobbed myself to sleep. I started to feel as if I was losing who I was. I was in trouble.

Richard and I continued to talk occasionally when I went to the pharmacy. Leaving the store to go next door and see his pleasant face became an escape for me. I was so happy that he had recommended going to school and getting my GED. I will forever be grateful to him. His calm and quiet spirit was so refreshing. He made me feel safe. Mr.'s trips out of town got more prolonged and more frequent, and during these trips, I took the opportunity to get to know more about Richard. We started spending more time together, meeting up at the pharmacy and talking. He made me feel beautiful and feminine. I was his equal when we were together. I was older by five years, but I felt as though he was more mature. We could talk for hours about everything or nothing at all. I shared how inconsistent Mr.'s emotions were and how it made me afraid at times. He would always comfort me with his wise words. Because of his kindness and his friendship, I was developing strong feelings for him that pushed our platonic friendship into a complicated space.

Months later, Mr. and I had yet another fight in the store regarding the same woman from the grocery store across the street. This time, he slapped me in the face. I ran out of the store, crying. I went to the pharmacy to get some headache medicine, hoping that Richard would not be there this time. But he was. He asked me what was wrong, and I told him through my sobs. He told me not to go back into the store and to take a bus and get off at the mall in downtown Philly and wait for him. I did as Richard instructed, and as I waited for him, all kinds of fears and thoughts ran through my mind. I wanted to stay and wait, but I also wanted to leave because I was afraid that Mr. would find me. Something made me stay and wait for Richard to meet me at the mall.

We spent the afternoon together, and for those few hours, it was just him and me. We ate, drank, walked around the mall, talked, and laughed. He made me forget about my problems and how unhappy and afraid I was at home. During those hours with Richard, time stood still. All I wanted was to be in the same space with this beautiful human being. During those few hours with Richard, I felt the most loved I had felt since leaving my home in Jamaica. Since moving in with the man I thought was my knight in shining armor.

As we said our goodbyes and boarded separate buses to our destination, I wondered if we would ever be able to do this again. I felt alive, but the moment I sat on the bus and headed home, my heart started racing. My palms were wet, and I was terrified to go back and face Mr. The overwhelming sadness of missing my daughter, my parents, my friends, and my family crept up on me. I cried as I sat on the bus, tears falling down my face. I had been in the States for a year, and I hated my life. I regretted moving from Jamaica—but I couldn't tell anyone. And I couldn't tell anyone about the abuse. I did not want them to worry.

When I got home, Mr. was not there. Thank God, I thought, with a sigh of relief. I missed the bullet this time around. We never discussed the incident that happened in the store, but I knew he was seeing that woman.

A few weeks later, Mr. was off on another trip to Texas. (He always claimed they were business trips, and I tried not to get involved.) I had had so much fun with Richard at the mall earlier that month that we decided to hang out again. I met up with him, and in the vulnerability of my fragile state, we became intimate. It was beautiful. He was gentle and passionate. I had not felt so wanted and so loved in a long time, but I knew we had crossed a dangerous line. I knew our intimacy would make things complicated. I was afraid of what would happen if Mr. found out about us. Richard did not deserve to be dragged into a triangle, and as much as he wanted to be in my life, I felt the need to protect him. The only way I knew how to do that was to end our friendship.

I never honestly told him why I stopped taking his calls and stopped calling him. I ended all communication with him, and my heart was sad. He was my only trusted friend outside of Dami, but I could not run the risk of anyone finding out about our special friendship. He was confused about the abrupt end. He tried desperately to talk to me, but I kept my distance. One day, he showed up across the street from my home, and I thought I was going to have a heart attack. Mr. was not there, so I went outside and told Richard never to do that again and never to try to contact me. He never argued with me, but I could see the hurt in his eyes as he slowly walked away and said, "I will always be here for you if you ever need me."

I walked back into the house and fell on my bed and cried.

CHAPTER SEVEN

HOPE DEFERRED

Dami would sometimes stay with her grandmother or her aunt, who was a positive force and role model in her life. But once I got into the picture, Dami spent most of her time with me. I loved Dami. She had become more than a daughter to me. She was my friend, my confidant. She had gone through a roller-coaster life. Her mom had gone away when she was three years old, and she had been living with her dad since then. She had also lived with several women who were in and out of her father's life. One woman in particular put her in a bathtub of hot water and burned her skin. That broke my heart and brought me to tears.

I noticed the differences in how my dad had treated me as a child and how Mr. treated Dami. His form of punishment for her—if she did something to upset him—was that she had to memorize a psalm a day. She would have to study it and recite it to him when he came home. I used to help her study because he expected her to say it without mistakes. I felt so sorry for her. Her eyes were always sad. I really wasn't sure how to be a mother to her, but I loved her enough to be whatever I could. We were each other's company. When we were alone, we had so much fun.

I got pregnant for the second time with Mr. I was happy about this one. I felt that this baby would take away the pain of missing Kay and would provide me with someone to love in this precarious existence. Since I no longer had Richard, my baby would give me all the love I was searching for and maybe bring Mr. and me closer together. I had a tough pregnancy and was often very ill. This didn't change Mr.'s habits of staying out all the time and coming home in the wee hours of the morning. My aunt came up to visit from Jamaica and stayed with me for a couple weeks during my pregnancy. I had morning sickness and stomach issues every day for the entire pregnancy. I threw up everything I ate. My aunt used to come into the bathroom with me with a wet towel and hold my head as I vomited. When my aunt left, Dami spent time with me, talking, laughing, telling me stories about school, and making sure I was okay.

The day of my delivery, Mr. and I went to the hospital. With my OBGYN on vacation, I was placed with a resident doctor who delivered the baby. The delivery was challenging. I was not given an epidural, and during the delivery process, I tore badly. The baby's left shoulder was stuck under the cervix. The doctors tried to get it out, but in the process, they damaged a nerve. I truly believed that if my OBGYN was present, or if another OBGYN—instead of a resident—delivered me in his practice, things would have turned out differently for my baby. They failed to implement the proper procedure for that type of difficult delivery. She weighed in at nine pounds, three ounces, and because of her size, there was a higher risk of injuries, which was not taken into account.

Mr. and I later learned that the damage to the nerve was called Erbs Palsy, but at the time of delivery, they were not sure what happened and why she was unable to move her left hand. When I found out they hurt my baby, I was devastated. For the first nine months of her life, my baby girl Shay could not move her left hand on her own, and her left arm was clearly shorter than her right arm. Dami loved Shay and helped me with her as much as she could. Shay was referred to physical and occupational therapy, and I had to perform specific exercises and techniques twice a day on her arm. I prayed over my little girl every day, and I believed in my heart that God would heal her. Shay eventually started moving her hand but never regained full mobility; the type of nerve damage she sustained can never be repaired.

My hopes that the baby would bring Mr. and me closer together were futile. Things got worse. We argued all the time over little things, and his verbal abuse was constant. I gained sixty pounds during my pregnancy, and I think Mr. was repulsed by the weight. I could not do anything right, and he nitpicked everything I did. But he loved his newborn daughter. When he held her, his eyes lit up, and it was as if he came alive. So often, I thought of leaving him, but I did not know where I would go. Now that I had a new baby, I had no choice but to stay. I convinced myself that I had to cope. I told myself that I needed to do everything in my power to please him so that we would stop fighting. I did everything imaginable to do that. I tried to lose the weight so he would look at me the way he did when I first came to live with him. When he was happy, I was delighted. It was no longer about me. I hid and became a shadow of who I once was. In doing so, I lost myself. I no longer knew who Joan was. I would not talk back to him if he got upset; I would keep quiet for the sake of peace. I wanted peace for my girls, Shay and Dami.

Four months after Shay was born, Mr. and I decided to get married. Although things were not ideal, I hoped that getting married would give us a sense of commitment and security, especially now that I had the baby, and Mr. loved her so much. In my mind, I thought this was what we needed to get closer. I did not like that our relationship was common-law because the sanctity of marriage was important to me. Another critical component of this was that it was essential for me to have my legal paperwork to file for Kay to come live with us. I also wanted to make sure Kay was coming to the United States and into a family dynamic. Mr. agreed, so we got engaged.

I am not sure if Mr.'s family knew what was happening between us regarding the abuse because I never told them, and Dami did not either. They assisted us with all the planning and preparations for the nuptials. I was extremely grateful. On the day of the wedding, we were surrounded by friends and family. I was happy to have my big sister Fay as my matron of honor, and one of my best friends from Jamaica, Althea, was my photographer. My big brother, Jeffrey, was also there. I was saddened by the fact that my mom and Kay were not there, but I knew that they were with me in spirit. I also wished my dad could have walked me down the aisle. Although I was still upset by his betrayal, I always loved him, and no one could replace him. I agreed to have Mr.'s brother-in-law walk me down the aisle.

As I was walking toward the front of the church, I felt a deep sense of doubt. I shuddered but quickly shifted my thoughts. Despite the rocky start we had, I was optimistic that this day would turn things around. The service and the reception were beautiful, and having Dami and Shay there made it even more special.

We had booked a hotel room for the wedding night, and I was looking forward to making love to my husband. It had been several months since we had been intimate, and I knew our wedding night would be beautiful. I wanted it to be. When we got to the hotel to settle in for the night, I went to the bathroom to freshen up and change into my sexy lingerie. As soon as I climbed into the bed, he turned his back to me and went to sleep. I was afraid to touch him for fear of being rejected, so I covered my face and cried in silence.

A man who turns his back on his wife on their wedding night is cold as ice and does not deserve her. When I could not cry anymore, I stared at the ceiling and asked God, why me? I felt ashamed and unwanted. Mr. slept the entire night with his back turned to me, woke up the next morning, and got dressed for us to leave. I changed and followed him to the car. We did not say one word to each other on the drive home. I felt discarded. I had once read that if you got married and did not consummate the marriage that night, then you could have it annulled. I thought about annulment but dismissed it, as I was too confused to think straight.

Five days after our wedding, my husband left home and was gone for an entire weekend without any explanation. I had no idea where he had gone. Dami asked where he was, but I had no answer for her. Something was not adding up. My instincts kicked in, and I started going through his stuff.

I was not sure what I was looking for, but I knew there had to be something going on. After several failed attempts to get in touch with Mr., I had Dami reach out to his cousin Ed, who usually knew his whereabouts. While Dami was calling Ed, I looked through papers and receipts that Mr. kept in a drawer. I found a phone bill and opened it up. I looked at all the numbers that were incoming and outgoing, and pretty soon, I was able to narrow down a few numbers that appeared quite frequently on the bill. I went into super sleuth mode. I circled the repetitive ones, and I was able to match up some of them to his family members. By this time, Dami had heard from Ed, who told her that Mr. was in Washington, DC. That was a change. What would he be doing in DC? I asked Dami to help me decipher the rest of the numbers on the phone bill. One particular number appeared over and over again, but what made it unique was the time of day the calls were made and received. Some were during the early morning and others were late at night, and they were for long periods. Whoever owned that number was engaging in lengthy conversations with my husband at various times of the day and night. I dialed, and my heart pounded as it rang. This was a Saturday night, precisely one week after my wedding.

"Hello?" came from the other end of the line.

I hesitated, and then the person repeated, "Hello?"

"Hi," I said. I told her I was just checking to see who the number belonged to because I noticed it was on my husband's phone bill several times.

She said, "Well, this is my number, and who is your husband?"

I told her his name.

All hell broke loose.

Lolita had just graduated high school. She lived in South Philadelphia—and she was having an affair with Mr. She told me that my husband was her man and that he would take her to school in the mornings and pick her up in the evenings. She said Mr. gave her a car as a gift. She had no idea that he had gotten married the previous weekend. She had noticed he was wearing a new ring on his finger, but he told her he had bought himself a gift. She said he never spoke about his newborn baby or me, but he had told her about Dami. Lolita shared with me that Mr. invited her to go with him to DC to hang out and go to a concert. She left no stone unturned. Now that she knew I was his wife, she wanted me to know everything about them. I never saw this one coming. Yes, I suspected that he was cheating, but not like this.

I had found out from Dami that when Mr. met me, he was in Jamaica on vacation to visit his family and brought one of his many girlfriends with him. As soon as he returned to the States, he dumped that girl. Then, a few days before I came to live with him, he told the woman he was living with to leave. Then there was the young woman who worked across the street from his store that we fought about. But now a high school senior? He was thirty-four years old—seven years older than me—but here he was, having an affair with an eighteen-year-old, and who knows for how long? I kept calling his number over and over, hoping he would answer. When he finally did, all I said to him was that I spoke to Lolita and she told me everything. He hung up the phone.

I kept calling back, but it kept ringing until it started going straight to voicemail. I did not hear back from my husband for the rest of that day. The walls of the house felt like they were crumbling around me. My ears were hot. I was a wreck. I was angry, I was jealous, and I felt sick, all at the same time. He destroyed every bit of hope I had for us, for our future, for my babies. I was conflicted. I was hoping for better. He was too occupied with someone else to be emotionally available to me on our wedding night. Dami tried to comfort me, but I had fallen apart. Nothing could console me. When I thought about my life at that point, I hated myself. I could hear the words of my mother in my head. *Do you really know him?* I wanted my mom. I needed to lay my head on her shoulder and sob. I wanted to hug Kay. I wept for the void of Shawn and Richard—men who had treated me well. My life was in total confusion. I had no idea how I would recover from this. Mr. had bought her a car, and I didn't have one! I had to rely on him to take me places, or I had to take public transportation, but Lolita had a brand new car. I could not get past that.

I was still breastfeeding during this time, and when I tried to feed my baby, the taste of the breast milk must have changed because, after one pull, she started screaming and refused to take the breast. I had to give her formula for the first time. I think the chemicals released into my body due to depression, tears, sadness, and stress had changed the taste of my breast milk.

Mr. came home the next day.

My eyes were still swollen from crying for hours the day prior. I had tried several times to call Lolita back, but she never answered. Finally, I got a recording that her number was changed. I am sure Mr. was the one who told her to change her number.

I was sitting in the dining room when he entered the house, and my tears started again. I could not control my emotions. All I thought about was what my dad had done to my mom. Now I am dealing with the same fate. Another betrayal! I started screaming and yelling at him. For the first time, I had no fear about what he might do to me. I did not care. I had to get out all that was inside me. A barrage of words projected from my lips through my broken voice and sobs.

"Why would you do this to me?"

"What have I ever done to you for you to treat me this way?"

"What has changed since I left Jamaica two years ago?"

"You told me I was your queen, who am I now?"

"Is this why you did not touch me on our wedding night, because of her?"

"How could you leave for days and not tell me where you were?"

"Why a teenager? You could be her father, isn't that a crime?"

"You bought her a car—a freaking car. I have a baby and do not own a car!"

"I am taking my baby and moving back to Jamaica!"

"I am done with you!"

"I am sorry I left my home and my daughter to come here and be with you!"

"My mom warned me, but I did not listen!"

"Go back to Lolita. I am buying a ticket today to go back home."

"I hate you!"

His response to all of that was a nervous chuckle. I was dumbfounded.

"Is that all you have to say?" I asked.

He finally said that she was lying. That everything she told me was a lie. He came up with some ridiculous story about the car he bought her and said to me that she no longer had the car. I could see the lies in his eyes as he tried to explain away the whole situation. He made up a story for every question I asked him. He had a rebuttal for everything that Lolita had shared with me. As I listened to him lie, I knew I would never know the full truth.

Dami was around when all of this happened, and she devastated for me. She tried everything in her power to console me, but I was inconsolable. I was lost, confused, and totally shattered. Mr. saw how bad of shape I was in, and he felt sorry for me. His eyes softened, and I saw compassion. He begged me to stop crying. I was surprised at how gentle and caring he was toward me. For a split second, I saw the great guy I met in Jamaica, and this is when I knew for sure he had two personalities. I was all cried out and exhausted with a splitting headache. I had not eaten in two days, and

I could feel my body shutting down. I was unable to breastfeed so my baby was forced to take the formula. She refused it most of the day, but she got so hungry that she reluctantly started drinking it.

As I walked upstairs to get some rest, Mr. told me he was sorry and he would make everything right. He told me he did not want me to go back home to Jamaica. He said he loved me and was sorry that she (Lolita) lied to me. I was too weak to respond at this point and crawled in the bed and fell asleep.

The next day, Mr. told me that he bought a car for me and was looking into buying a home for us in New Jersey, so we could leave Philadelphia. He said he needed a change of scene. I was reluctant to believe anything he said at this point, but I stayed calm in response. I had woken up with a headache and felt like I was in a fog. I was still contemplating moving back to Jamaica, but there was so much to process, and I was not up for the challenge.

That day, Mr. was exceptionally kind and attentive. He made dinner for us and tried his best to make the mood in the house lighter. He loved on his baby girl and was even more playful with Dami. He told me he was sorry that I had to experience the lies of someone who wanted to destroy him. He said he was just a friend to her and was trying to help her because she was going through a tough time. He claimed that taking her to school was just to help her, but that was all. I was still too exhausted and empty to engage in any conversations. All I did was listen, knowing that he was feeding me a bunch of lies.

The next day, he left the house for a couple hours, and when he came back, he called me to go outside. And what do you know? Sitting in front of our townhome was a brand new red Suzuki convertible SUV. He said it was a gift for me. I knew deep down that he took the car from Lolita to get me this vehicle. But I did not care. He got caught, and this was his way of trying to right the wrong. I was delighted that I had my own ride, finally. Independence, here I come, I thought. I did not have my US driver's license and, truth be told, I was very nervous about driving on the highways, so Mr. hired a driving instructor to help me, and shortly after, I was driving around in my new ride.

Mr. bought us a beautiful single-family home in the suburbs of New Jersey. It was everything I could have ever dreamed of and then some: four bedrooms, three bathrooms, formal living and dining rooms, a sunken family room, a breakfast kitchen, front and back porches, custom window treatments, a two-car extended garage, and a swimming pool. I was happy. We settled into our beautiful home, and things were going well. Mr. and I were getting along much better than we were in Philly. We spent a lot of time shopping for the right furniture and household accessories to customize our home. I started to feel that things were turning around for the best, and I put the past behind me. Our new home brought a sense of security and fulfillment.

Approximately one year later, my daughter Kay joined us in New Jersey. She was now eight years old. The day we picked her up from the airport, I wrapped my arms around my beautiful firstborn. I hugged and kissed her and told her how much I loved and missed her. It had been four years since the last time I held her in my arms, and now my life was complete. All the years of crying for her and feeling empty were gone. She had grown so much. Her hair was long and beautiful, and the soft hair at the nape of her neck and around her forehead was slightly blond. She looked at me, her eyes filled with questions. It was almost as if she did not recognize me. She touched my face and my hair and asked, "Are you . . . my mommy?"

I said, "Yes, baby, don't you remember me?"

"You look different," she replied.

I certainly looked different. I had blond, curly hair—a big difference from my hair in Jamaica—and I also had a toddler, her sister, Shay.

CHAPTER EIGHT

A LEOPARD NEVER CHANGES ITS SPOTS

My older half-brother (my mother's child) was living in New York and filed for my mother to live in the United States permanently. I was so happy she got to leave Jamaica and all the scandal of my father's infidelity with it. My younger brother and sister also made the move to New York, so I did not feel as isolated anymore. After all, New York was a short trip from New Jersey, and knowing that I had family close by, I felt more secure. Life was looking up for me, and I was able to relax. Mr. also seemed more relaxed and was not as verbally or emotionally abusive. I started to let my guard down.

I enrolled Kay into elementary school, but it was a difficult adjustment for her. It took a while for her to get acclimated to the new country, new home, new little sister, and new stepfather. She missed my mom and my sister, who had been her caretakers for the past four years. I tried my best to make her as happy as I could under the circumstances, making sure that Mr. did not revert to his old ways in her presence.

Things seemed to be going well for the most part, but Mr. was very particular about the house. He would walk around with a cleaning rag and wipe any spot he saw on the wall or floor. He got so obsessive about the cleanliness that we were afraid to touch the walls. I tried my best to monitor the girls to make sure that they did not mess anything up. Except when we were having dinner, Dami mostly kept to herself and stayed in her room.

My brother and sister came to visit a few times, and when they were there, things were almost perfect. Mr. was always in the best of moods and was a lot of fun. He liked my brother and sister, and they got along well. We would sometimes go out and have fun together. When they were around, Mr. was super nice to me. I saw the best of him during those times, and it made me happy. My daughter Kay loved having her uncle and aunt there. She enjoyed their company, and it was awesome to see the smile in her eyes.

My brother stayed with us for a while because we had the accommodations, and one day, he had a big blowup with Mr., which surprised me. I did not know the whole story or why it happened at that time. I wasn't made aware of the truth until several years later. But when I felt as if my brother was disrespecting my husband in our home, I asked him to leave. My brother was devastated that his own sister put him out of her home, knowing that he did not have another place to go in New Jersey. But in my defense, I did not want to rock the boat and mess up the peace that was in my home at that time. I felt I had to side with my husband. It broke my heart to see my brother go.

Things changed between Mr. and me after my brother left. With my family no longer there, he reverted back to his abusive self. By this time, Dami was in high school and Kay was in elementary school. Shay, the baby, was around eighteen months old and running around being her bubbly, happy self. Mr. started staying out later and later, and when I asked him about his whereabouts, he would get agitated, so I stopped asking him. The health food store that he owned was not doing well as a business. He was not making a profit, and there were times he would close the store in the daytime and leave to do other things. That lack of consistency was terrible for a business, and there was also the competition with other well-known health food chains that were stifling the success of his small establishment. I stopped working at the store after Shay was born, and Mr. eventually closed it down.

To help with the bills, I got a temporary part-time job at a department store. I was so happy to be able to get a break from the house when I was at work. A few months later, the temporary part-time job turned into a permanent part-time job, and I felt a sense of independence. Before I secured employment, I was at the mercy of Mr. feeding us, clothing us, and paying all the bills. There was a period during that time when I owned only one pair of black jeans and a long sweater jacket. During the winter months, I wore the same clothes over and over until the black jeans turned gray and the long sweater was frayed at the elbows and sleeves. I was embarrassed. Besides that sweater, I owned a faux fur coat, which Mr. had bought for me years earlier, but I could not wear that casually. I went through an entire winter in New Jersey wearing a long sweater as a coat. Dami, on the other hand, was so tired of wearing the same old outfits to school that she started ripping things apart and putting them together to create new outfits and a new look for school. It was easier for me to get things for Kay and Shay because I could shop at discount stores. I would go without, so they had what they needed. Unlike the rest of us, Mr. always had new outfits. He stayed sharp in the latest shoes and clothes, but we were lacking. The job that I got at the department store changed that.

Yet we continued to walk around the house on eggshells. At the end of each night, I would check the walls and floors to make sure there were no fingerprints or spots anywhere. He would inspect the house when he came home, and there would be cussing and fussing if it was not up to his standard. Besides criticizing us for the house's condition, he stayed to himself, living in isolation and spending all his time watching TV. We rarely did anything together as a family. He managed to separate Shay and Kay and prevented them from playing together. I knew that Kay felt isolated, but I did not know how to change that. Dami was getting quieter and more withdrawn when she was home. She always seemed sad.

Then it happened. One particular morning, Dami went to the school bus carrying more bags than usual, and her book bag seemed heavier. But I didn't give it a second thought. That evening, she did not come off the bus. She never came back. She had run away for good. I was devastated, I was hurt, I was disappointed that she was unable to confide in me. We had gotten so close, but I never knew how to change her unhappiness. I felt as if I had let her down. The next morning, I talked to our neighbor and one of Dami's classmates, who she had become really close friends with. She told me that Dami had gone to stay in Philly with her mother, with whom she was recently united. Mr. did not try to get her. He said because she had left, she should stay out there and not come back. She was his firstborn daughter, and he did not care. I cried for my Dami. I did not see her again until a decade later.

With Dami gone, I think Mr. felt the need to forge a relationship with his sons, whom he never brought around. One day, he went to get the younger one to come to the house so he could spend time with him. Mr. picked him up in the afternoon, dropped him off at the house, and said he would be right back. He didn't come back until late evening, when it was time to take his son home. I was angry because he left him with me and I did not know how to keep him occupied or entertained. I had not been given a chance to have a relationship with either of Mr. sons. Furthermore, it was supposed to be a bonding moment between a father and son. But that never happened. There was definitely a pattern to his behavior with his children.

Mr. was getting more controlling with Kay. She had to stay in her room most of the time, and she would not get to play with her sister as much as she wanted to. He isolated her. She was not used to being locked inside a house when she was not in school. Her freedom as she knew it in Jamaica was restricted, and she did not like that. Mr.'s reasons for her not going outside were never clear. It was just his rule, and we had to abide by it.

On some days when I was at work, he would take Shay on the road with him and leave Kay all alone at home. She was not allowed to watch TV or make any noise when he was not there, for the fear that someone might think she was home alone. My poor daughter, who was surrounded by all the love in the world in Jamaica, was brought into a life of loneliness because her mother, having all the right intentions, brought her into it. The guilt consumed me. One day, he was so upset with her that he shook her, and she got so scared that she peed on herself. I felt helpless. I felt like I had betrayed my own child the same way my dad had betrayed my mother and the same way my husband had betrayed me. I could not get the word "betrayal" out of my heart or out of my life.

***

One day while I was at work, I looked up, and there in front of me stood Richard, from the pharmacy. I was so happy to see him. We talked for a little, but because I was at work, we planned to meet up later to talk in private. We met during the day at a local hotel, where no one knew either of us, so we would have some privacy and could spend as much time as possible catching up. I came clean with Richard and told him why I had to end our friendship abruptly. I wanted him to know that it was for his protection and my safety. He understood. He told me that he wanted to see me in person to tell me he was getting married. He had graduated from college with his degree in pharmacy, and he was marrying his girlfriend. I was happy for him but felt a wave of sadness, knowing that this may be the last time we ever saw each other. I congratulated him and wished him all the best. What a lucky girl, I thought. She was getting an incredible guy who would be a dream husband. I felt a tinge of jealousy and wished that I had met him under different circumstances.

At some point while we were in the room talking, I heard a lot of noise and commotion outside. Someone was knocking on random room doors asking if their wife was in any of the rooms with a man. I recognized the voice and froze. Mr. was trying to get the hotel staff to tell him if I was there, but the room was in Richard's name and he did not know anything about him. He was asking for my name, and the hotel was unable to give him any information. Mr. decided that since the hotel was not giving him any information, he was going to call the police for them to get me out because he knew I was there. He'd seen my car in the parking lot. The cops came, and while they were outside talking, Richard slipped out of the room without being seen, walked to the lobby, and sat incognito. I stayed in the room, and once the cops calmed Mr. down, I came out of the room alone. I told the cops that I had wanted to spend some time by myself, so I decided to rent a room and relax for a few hours. Mr. almost got in trouble because he called law enforcement under false pretenses. The police officers were able to calm Mr. down and diffuse the situation. I got in my car and drove home. Mr. never talked about the incident. I'm sure he was suspicious, but I stuck to my story. That was the last time I ever saw or heard from Richard.

***

One day, a tow truck pulled up in our driveway, hooked up to the red car Mr. had given me, and took it away. I had no idea Mr. was not paying the car payments. He was so irate that the car got repossessed, he could not see straight. He was upset with me for not contributing enough toward the household, and that now he had to take me to work.

Mr. was getting more volatile, and I was becoming more afraid of him. He wanted me to use all my part-time money toward paying bills. I was making $6.50 per hour and only working twenty hours per week. I could not afford to pay the gas bill or the phone bill, which were my responsibilities. To punish me, he allowed the gas and the phone to be disconnected. Because of this, I became very resourceful. Once when he left for another trip to Texas, I bought a one-burner electric stove so I could cook for my daughters and myself. I found a pay phone that was about half a mile away, and I walked to use the pay phone if I needed to talk to someone.

Kay also became resourceful. Mr. did something to the TV plug that was in her room to prevent her from watching it. She used a knife and rigged the wires together to get the TV working. He would go to her room to check the top of the TV, but she would put ice on the top to cool it down while she watched it so he could never tell.

The verbal and psychological abuse happened almost daily and was more frequent and damaging than the physical abuse. I felt in my heart that something was off with Mr., but I did not want to ask his family any questions for fear they would tell him that I was snooping around. I was afraid to let my family know what I was going through. When he was not home, the girls and I had the most fun. We would sit in the California King bed in my bedroom and eat pizza.

One Christmas, I was scouted and chosen to attend a live audition to do a print ad for Lane Bryant. I was ecstatic. I told Mr. about it, and he seemed happy for me. The day of the audition came, and he told me he was on his way to take me there. I got dressed up, did my own makeup, and sat there and waited . . . and waited . . . and waited. When I realized that it was getting late, I called him repeatedly, but he never answered his phone. He showed up eight hours later. I had missed the audition and the opportunity. When I asked him why he did not come to get me for the audition, he said they were just trying to exploit me. I told him that he should have said that before telling me he was on his way. I despised him for this. His goal was to control me.

In an effort to bring in more money, I applied for a full-time job with the department store I was working at and got it. I immersed myself into my new job, and I excelled. Mr. still hated the fact that he had to take me to and from work five days out of the week, and he would always be late, whether taking me into work or coming to get me. I got smart and started to lie about my start and end times so that I would get to work and leave on time. Sometimes he would come to pick me up with Shay in the car. She would be so happy to see me when I got in the car and would try to get up and hug me. He would reach his hand behind him, grab her, and push her back in the backseat, so she could not hug me. She would let out a whimper and cry silently. I would look through the passenger side rear view mirror and see tears running down her face. When I would ask him, "Why are you hurting her?," he would slap me across the face with the back of his hand. I would cry in silence, my heart breaking for my daughter and what she was witnessing and experiencing. This happened on several occasions. He also threatened to drive the car off the bridge so we would all die. He would drive at speeds up to a hundred miles per hour and would drive on the shoulders of the highway just to scare us.

There was one day in particular when I was done working at 6 p.m., and I called Mr. to let him know I was ready to leave. He was at home, and he said he'd be on his way. It was a Sunday, and the mall closed at 6:30 p.m. I sat outside and waited. I waited for two hours, and he still didn't come. By 8.30 p.m., the mall security had driven around the mall what seemed like a hundred times.

The security officer finally got out of his car and said, "Young lady, you've been sitting out here for two hours. Who are you waiting for?"

"I'm waiting on my husband," I said. "I called him several times and he kept telling me he was on his way. He should be here in ten minutes."

"Okay," said the security guard, and drove away.

At 9 p.m., Mr. was still not there. When I saw the lights of the security car coming back, I hid behind the bushes because I was too embarrassed for him to see me still waiting. I did not know who to call or what to do. It was dark, and I was all alone. As I hid behind the bushes, nervous and scared, my sorrow got the best of me. I broke down. I had no choice but to wait on this cruel man. Behind the bushes, I went into my bag and took out my journal, a gift from one of my friends at work. I wrote:

July 17

Oh, Lord, I don't know where I am. I don't know what is happening to me and where I'm going in life, but I'm leaving it all in your hands. Sometimes I feel like throwing my hands in the air and giving in, but then I remember Shay and Kay and I know I can't do that. I would honestly like to get an apartment on my own and to live alone with my two kids and without my husband. I know I might not be able to pay their rent and the utilities, but I just want to be alone. I could honestly do better than how I'm doing right now if I was on my own. I'm still feeling a little sick. I've been having a terrible headache all day. I really feel it is tension or something. It is getting late. I've been waiting for him for 2 and a half hours. I'm tired of the mall security driving around and seeing me here. If he stays much longer, I don't know what I'm going to do. I am the only one out here and I want to go home. I am hungry and I am tired. Lord, please give me the strength to cope with this life, to cope with the nagging, the fighting, the beating, with going to work late, with waiting long hours for him to pick me up, with him coming home at daybreak. You said in your good book that you won't give your children more than they could bear, but this is unbearable. I break down sometimes and cry and I wonder if you hear me. Please listen to me, Lord, and work something out for me. I beg you. Please give me a little break. I have taken enough. I do not know how much more I can take. Thank you, Lord. Everything that I have written here is the God's honest truth. Help me, Lord, to make the right decisions. Help me to make the right moves. Provide a car for me because that's the most important thing for me right now. How could I go about getting a car? Maybe I could sell something. Maybe I could ask each of my family members for 40 dollars. Oh, God, I don't know, but please show me a way. Give me a sign. I am waiting on you, Lord. Thanks. Joan.

Mr. showed up at 9:15 p.m., almost three hours late. He showed no concern of whether or not I was safe by myself at the mall, on a Sunday, when all the stores had been closed for hours. As he drove me home, I sat in silence, hugging the journal to my heart, tears streaming down my face. His heart was cold.

CHAPTER NINE

MY SILENT CRY FOR HELP

I'd had enough. I was sick of him referring to me as stupid and dirty. I was sick of not getting any affection from him. I was sick of appeasing him, laughing when he laughed just to stay on his good side. No matter how hard I tried to keep us at peace, he would get angry and criticize me and Kay. I felt like I was losing my mind. I wanted to get away. I wanted to leave but did not know how. I wrote in my journal.

October 21

Dear Lord, where are you?? Why, why, why have you left me here? I am broken, abused, and all alone. He has isolated us. How can I leave? Please send someone to help me. Please, God. I am afraid to tell anyone what is happening to me. I never saw this type of life at home. How did I get here? Is this punishment for me because of the life I lived in Jamaica? What did I do to deserve this? Kaydene is sad and unhappy and that is killing me. I don't know how to fix it because I did it to her. He is always taking Shay wherever he goes, as if to deliberately separate her from her sister! I am failing my kids. I have destroyed our lives. There is no one I can turn to for help.

While Mr. was away, and without his knowledge, I packed up with my children and took a cab to the train station to go to New York to stay with my sister. As we were sitting in the train station, he came walking in. My heart almost stopped. At the top of his lungs, he screamed at me and told me that I was kidnapping his daughter. He came over to me, grabbed my baby out of my hands, took the bag I had, and walked away. I screamed and cried in the train station, begging for help, but nobody came to help me. Some people turned their backs, and others ignored me. I ran behind him with Kay, so I would not be away from my baby girl. I knew what would happen when I got back home, but I was willing to go home and take the beating—if it came to that—because I was not going to let him take my baby daughter from me.

On the way home in the car, he was silent, and I was scared to death of what he would do. But when we got home, he asked us to get out of the car and told me to never attempt to take his daughter anywhere without his knowledge. The girls and I got out of the car and walked into the house. Mr. drove away. I breathed a sigh of relief as the tears ran down my face. I knew I was trapped.

Mothers are created with a special intuition, and they know when something is wrong in the lives of their children. They feel it in their soul. Shortly after the incident at the train station, my mom called and asked if she could visit. I said absolutely. I really wanted her to come and live with me, but I knew that would not fly with Mr. My mom had not seen me or Kay in a while. With my mom there, I felt safe. I knew Mr. would not act up. But I was wrong.

One day, we were sitting on the couch in the living room. Mom was sitting beside me, and Mr. started a conversation with me that got a little intense. He was getting upset, and when he got like this, profanity spewed from his lips. I was trying to explain my point of view, and he got irate. He hated when I responded to him. He wanted me to just listen and not speak because it gave him total power and control. But on this day in question, I was standing up for myself. He said that I was getting too mouthy and showing out because my mother was there. He went to the kitchen sink, turned on the hot water, filled a pan, walked it over to where I was sitting beside my mom, and dumped the water on me in front of her.

My mother was in shock. With tears in her eyes, she looked at him and said, "What if the water was hotter?"

"It would just burn her up," he said to her.

My mother was so devastated that she called my brother and left the next day. If Mr. could demonstrate that type of anger in front of her, then what was he doing to me when no one was watching? When my mother left, I knew I was in trouble. She and I never talked about that incident until years later. I felt as if she was too embarrassed for me to discuss it while I was still living with him.

The next time Mr. abused me, he kicked me during a fight. I fell down the stairs and hit my head at the bottom of the front door. I lay there for a while, pretending I was passed out. He called 911, and an ambulance came to take me to the emergency room. While we were at the hospital, I was hoping I could tell someone I was being abused. But Mr. stood at my bedside with Shay while a cop questioned me on the other side of the bed. I think the hospital staff suspected domestic violence when I got checked in, hence the cop. As he was asking me questions, I got the feeling he was almost begging me to tell him that my husband was the one who hurt me. But when I saw my baby in Mr.'s hands and knew that Kay was home alone, I was too afraid of child protective services getting involved and taking my children, so I lied and told the cop I fell.

How could a trained police officer put me on the spot like that? Could he not see the fear in my eyes or hear the tremble in my voice? How could he miss the intimidating way Mr. was looking at me?

***

Even with the chaos going on in my life, I applied to nursing school because I wanted a career. I wanted to make something of myself in this country, and I did not think that retail would provide that for me. I wanted to be able to get away and provide for my girls. I was really excited when I got accepted. This was the opportunity for me to finally get my degree.

When Mr. found out that I had applied to college and got in, he was not happy. He said he would not take on the responsibility of driving me to and from class. He told me that if I did go back to school, I would have to leave. But I knew that would mean I would have to leave my daughter Shay, and he knew I would never go without her. At that time, I had no resources, no out, and no idea where I would go or how I would take care of my children if I left. If I stayed, at least I knew we would have a roof over our heads and food on the table. So for the second time in my life, I gave up the dream of having a secondary education.

I was trapped in a physically, verbally, financially, spiritually, and psychologically abusive nightmare. I felt like I was going crazy. I started looking in the yellow pages for women's shelters, hoping to get some help to leave him. But I was so angry when I received the shelter information in the mail. I knew that any means of communication would have been risky, but I gave them my work number, and that would have been a safer way to communicate with me than sending the letter to my home. What if Mr. had seen it? I ripped up the letter and never called them again.

It had been two years since Mr. and I were intimate when he came home one night and walked straight to the bedroom. I was shocked that he crawled in the bed with me. It was customary for him to come home at dawn and sleep in the den. On this night, however, he came into the bed and, without any gentleness or foreplay, he took off my underwear and had sex with me. When he was done, he got up without any care as to whether or not I was satisfied. That one night resulted in a pregnancy. Six weeks later, when I told him I was pregnant, he suggested that I get an abortion. I was not sad that he wanted me to have an abortion because God knows I did not want to bring another child into the world under the circumstances that I found myself in. So I complied. He took me to get the procedure done and, in my heart, I knew it was over. I was done with him. But I still did not know how I was ever going to leave.

Mr. became more and more unpredictable. There was a young lady who showed up at our home one day, and he told me that she was involved in a business venture with him. The shocking thing was that I knew her from Jamaica. We had gone to high school together. I never quite got what type of work she did for him, but I stopped trying to pry into his secret life. I left it alone. Shortly after she left, it appeared that he was in hiding. Something was wrong. He started staying home, and he would keep the doors locked and the blinds closed even in the daytime. He placed a cabbage on top of the refrigerator to ward off evil, and he wouldn't allow anyone to touch it. I did not understand the significance of the cabbage, and I dared not ask him why it was important for him to do that. He would tell me on occasion that people were trying to kill him. I was living a nightmare.

This got me to my darkest day.

***

To that point when I wanted to take my life and the lives of my daughters. But God. He showed up for me, and look at who He used—the baby. I marveled at her intelligence at only three and a half years old. I immediately felt a deep desire to live for them and for me, but I also felt as deep of a disappointment for getting to such a low point. What was I thinking? Why was I ready to give up and take the lives of my innocent children? Why would I want to end their lives without giving them any options? I was the one who chose to be there; it was up to me to fix it. I knew there had to be a better life than this one. God did not bring me through the *sands of the desert* for me to go out like this.

I got up from the floor, got dressed, and woke my older daughter. We all went downstairs for breakfast. I grabbed my journal and started writing. This time, there was hope in my writing. God had given me another chance. I remembered reading a scripture in Habbakuk that said, "Write the vision, and make it plain." I was going to be very clear and specific in my writing to get what I needed in life. Writing became my motivation to survive. It became comfort and fuel for my soul. The pages in my journal started to paint the picture of a life I desired.

CHAPTER TEN

A CHOICE

With my newfound enlightenment, I turned to faith. Every night before going to bed, my girls and I sat in my bed and read Psalms 91. I would read it and they would repeat it. It was as if we were summoning the angels from heaven to descend down and rescue us. My favorite lines were verses 4–6: "He will cover thee with his feathers, and under his wings shalt thou trust: his truth shall be thy shield and buckler. Thou shalt not be afraid for the terror by night; nor for the arrow that flieth by day; Nor for the pestilence that walketh in darkness; nor for the destruction that wasteth at noonday" (KJV). I knew without a doubt that God heard our prayers and was setting His plans in motion. But it would take one last collision with Mr. to push me completely over the edge.

A few days later, I got a page from a long-time friend who I knew back in Jamaica. When I called him, it was so nice to hear his voice. After the initial "hi," "hello," "it's been a long time," he asked me how I was doing. I told him I was being abused by my husband and I didn't know what to do or how to leave. He told me to pack up my kids and leave. I told him I was afraid, and I would need to find a job. But he assured me that if I left, he would do his best to help me get settled in a new place. For some reason those words planted a seed of hope.

The following Wednesday morning, I was getting Kay ready to get on the school bus.

"Mommy, I have no lunch money," she said.

"What did you do with your money?" I asked.

"I can't find it."

"You have to be more careful," I said.

I usually give her ten dollars every Monday, as lunch was two dollars per day. On this day, she should have had six dollars left, but she had none. Mr. overheard the conversation and jumped in and said she was lying. I asked him why would she lie and I ignored the rest of his rants. I searched her pockets and book bag and could not find any money. I told her I would give her two dollars for that day and help her look for the rest of the money when I came home from work. Mr. commanded me to not give her any money for lunch to teach her a lesson, so she would be more careful next time. But I would not let my child go to school without money for lunch and stay hungry all day. She was an eleven-year-old, she was still my baby, and as a mother, I refused to do that to her. In my heart, I knew Mr. did not love her as a daughter or he would have never told me to send her to school without the means to eat lunch. He kept arguing with me and insisted that I send her to school without money. I walked away from him, took two dollars out of my purse, gave it to my daughter, and accompanied her to the bus stop. I waited until the bus left and went back into my house to get ready for work.

Shay was up and sitting in my bed, and Mr. was in the bathroom. I entered the bedroom, smiled at my baby, and proceeded to the bathroom to get ready.

His fist connected to my face.

I screamed and asked him, "Why did you hit me?"

"You disrespected me in front of Kay," he said. "You disobeyed me and gave her money."

Feeling extremely scared and threatened, I said to him softly, "I cannot let my child be at school and stay hungry all day. She is only eleven. She has never lost her money before."

I was almost whimpering at this point, holding my face, trying not to aggravate him anymore, knowing that my baby was sitting on the bed and had seen him hit me. Before I knew it, he was pounding me with his fist. I was screaming and trying to cover my face with my hands as he kept trying to find a way to get to my face with his fists. As I was trying to get out of the close quarters and into the bedroom, I slipped on the bathroom floor. I tried to break my fall by grabbing onto the sink and caught a glimpse of myself in the mirror. I was bleeding. I kept screaming in the hopes he would stop, and I heard my baby screaming too. He was using his fist with the ring on his finger, and he was specifically aiming at my face. I managed to get out of the bathroom and into the bedroom. I picked up the phone on the nightstand to call 911. He came up behind me, grabbed the phone out of my hand, and ripped the phone jack out of the wall, taking dry wall with it. Shay was crying and begging him to stop.

The next words he said to me sent chills down my spine. "If you call the cops in my house, I will kill you and be happy to spend the rest of my life in prison."

When I looked into his eyes, his pupils were black. I saw evil and I shuddered. At that moment, I heard the smallest whisper.

"Don't talk, Mommy, don't talk," my sweet baby said.

I looked at her and saw that she was afraid for me. I picked her up and sobbed with her in my arms. I knew he would not hit me while I was holding her. He screamed at me to put her down, and I did. But I heard her request, asking me not to speak, and I never said another word. He carried on with his rant and rage. I knew my child's words to me were to say, if you talk, he will be angry and keep hitting you, so don't say anything. I fixed my gaze on her. I was bleeding and trembling, tears running down my face as I looked at our daughter. He did not hit me again, but he kept saying, "If you had just listened to me and taught her a lesson, this would not happen." Finally, he stormed out of the bedroom and went downstairs.

That day I saw my life flash in front of my eyes. I knew one day his rage would get the best of him and I could lose my life. How could he be so angry at me for giving Kay two dollars for lunch? It broke my heart into tiny pieces. Standing there, half-dressed for work, totally broken and devastated by what had happened, I felt the weight of sorrow for my daughters. How can I kill him? I thought. Maybe I can wait until he is sleeping and pour hot cooking oil into his ear. That would take him out. But that thought soon disappeared because I had watched too much of the O. J. Simpson trial to know that the investigation would lead right back to me and I would be convicted, leaving my children to suffer in a world that had shown me so much cruelty. Who would protect and love them as much as me?

I was never a fighter. I was never good at conflict or physical altercations. I was always a peacemaker. I never liked to see people cuss at each other. Some would call me a scaredy cat or a wuss, but I was okay with that. Growing up, I would run away from anything that involved a fist fight. I avoided these situations my whole life and still somehow I ended up here. I spaced out as I stood by my bed shaking, and in that moment, the seed of flight was planted. My girls did not deserve to see this type of life. I could not raise them to think that this was okay. I knew how nervous they got when he came home. I got nervous too. I was tired of the fights, the slaps, the cussing, the verbal abuse, the way he looked at me and talked down to me. The words he sometimes used to describe me and how it would cut right through my heart. The profanities that he so loosely threw around without a care that the children could hear them.

I also thought about those occasional days when things were great. He had the most amazing laugh and a great sense of humor. When he was in a good mood, life seemed almost perfect, and it made me forget he had this other side. But the roller coaster of the bad outweighed the good, and after five years of more downs than ups, I harbored feelings of animosity toward him. I had to choose my girls.

I got dressed, and he reluctantly took me to work. Due to all the chaos that happened earlier, I was late again. When I got out of the car, I felt as if I was walking underwater in a plastic bubble. Everything was spinning, and my ears were ringing. I had a massive migraine from all the crying and screaming, and my face was swollen from where his fist had landed. I put my oversized sunglasses on and walked into my job to sign in at security. What I did not know was that there was blood on the blouse I wore to work. The security guard in charge asked me what had happened to me, and I responded that I was okay.

"Don't lie to me," he said. "You have blood on your shirt."

I took my sunglasses off and glanced down. Seeing the blood, I knew I could not lie anymore. That's when I lost my balance and almost collapsed. The security guard came around to the outside of the counter and grabbed me to prevent me from falling. He told me he was going to walk with me to my manager's office so I could get myself together. I was in no shape to provide great service to any customers at that point. As he walked with me to the office, I sobbed. There were so many emotions going through me. I was ashamed, embarrassed, hurt, overwhelmed with sadness for my daughters, and filled with hate. Yes—I hated him! When Mr.'s eyes had turned black, there was a transference of the hate in his heart into my spirit. We got to my manager's office, and for the first time in almost six years, I opened up and told every detail of what I was experiencing.

PART II

CROSSROADS

CHAPTER ELEVEN

THE PLAN

"Please, allow me to help you, Joan."

My manager's name was Korrin, and she showed compassion and empathy as I told her what I had been experiencing with Mr. She was one of the angels God sent to help me, and I owe her a debt of gratitude that I will never be able to repay.

Although I was going through such a difficult time at home—there were many times I went to work with sadness in my eyes or a tear-stained face—whenever the store doors opened, I changed into the most dynamic and energetic employee. During the work hours, I immersed myself in the job and completely shut out my reality. As soon as the work day was over, my heart started palpitating and my palms started sweating because I did not know if I was going home to Dr. Jekyll or Mr. Hyde. It was an arduous way to live. My coworkers knew that something was wrong in my personal life, but no one ever asked me to tell them what was going on, and I was too prideful to voluntarily share. Somehow, I never wanted them to think bad things about my husband or try to get the authorities involved and disrupt our lives. It was very strange that I thought about it that way. I guess I wanted the assistance to find a way out and leave without him having to be affected by the law. I remembered his threat to me about calling the cops on him, so I preferred not to get them involved.

Now here I was, letting it all out on the table as I shared with Korrin the roller coaster life I was living. I felt safe in her office and around her. I told her what had transpired earlier between Mr. and me. I knew it was time for someone to know the truth. I had lied so many times to the point where I had forgotten some of the lies I told to cover up my abuse.

Sitting in Korrin's office and feeling free to talk, I felt the need to go back in time to paint the picture of how I got there. As I shared my story with her, I started to see things from a different vantage point, and it was as if my eyes opened and things became clear to me. I told her how Mr. wooed me with his intense idealization. He told me I was his queen because I was born on the same day as his then idol, Haile Selassie, the Ethiopian Emperor. He said I was perfect in his eyes, and I was everything he needed in a woman. But that was an exaggeration. After living with him for some time, his personality split, and I no longer fulfilled the ideal role he had created in his mind about me, so he began to devalue me. He belittled me with his words, he ignored me for days at a time, and he refused to have sex with me for two years. He sabotaged my entry into the Lane Bryant model call and prevented me from going back to school. Whenever he was angry and out of control, it got physical.

As I was sharing with Korrin, I realized I was talking to myself. It hit me that Mr. was a narcissist and that, at the core of his narcissistic behavior, he was a man with a combination of entitlement, lack of self-love, and low self-esteem. The problem was never me; it was always him.

Korrin quietly listened and took notes while I poured my heart out. When I finished saying all I needed to say, she asked me if I had family anywhere in the States outside of New Jersey. I mentioned my older half-sister in Miramar, Florida. She picked up her phone and dialed a number. I thought my heart was going to stop when she put the phone on speaker and I heard the male voice on the other end of the line say, "Human Resources." Oh my god, I thought. Am I really going to get the help I need to leave?

Korrin shared the details of our conversation with the HR director on the other end of the line. He was very empathetic and told us that he would do everything in his power to assist me. He asked us to wait for a moment as he placed the call on hold. During the pause, Korrin told me to get a pen and paper and write what she was about to share with me. I rummaged around in my handbag and found a pen and my journal. But before she could tell me what she was going to say, the HR director came back on the line. What he said changed my life.

"I do have a full-time position available in the Aventura Store, however, it is not in cosmetics. Joan, we will hold the position for you until you can get here. Korrin, please give her my number, and Joan, whenever you get to Florida, please give me a call and we will get you situated in the store. I also noticed that you have some vacation time still left for the year. Please feel free to take that time to get relocated and settled."

I had no words! I did not know how to respond.

My mind started racing. Wait a minute, I thought, how am I going to leave? I had no plans. How do I just get up and go? What do I tell my sister in Florida? Will she be able to accommodate us? How do I make my escape without Mr. finding out? I could not believe it all was happening so fast. This was the moment I had prayed for. I had pleaded with God as I wrote in my journal daily. But now that He had answered my prayers, fear gripped me in the throat. I felt paralyzed.

"Joan? Joan, how does that sound?" The director's question startled me back to reality.

I was so overcome with emotions, I started sobbing.

"Thank you, thank you so much. I don't know what to say except that you just saved my life and the life of my daughters."

Korrin, seeing that I was a complete nervous wreck, thanked the HR director and said she'd get back to him after finishing up with me.

She hung up the phone and asked, "Are you ready to take notes?"

"Yes," I said.

"Do you have an idea as to when you want to leave?".

That was a question I did not have an answer to. I fumbled around in my mind trying to think it through.

"I don't know," I answered.

We were right smack in the biggest season of the year in retail. It was the fourth quarter, and for a fragrance associate, it was the highest-paid commission time of the year. I wanted to work through the holidays to secure a little savings so I could have some room to tie us over when left. The transfer came with the same benefits I currently had because my tenure and full-time status would stay intact. That included my health insurance and paid vacation time for the number of years I had already worked for the company.

I told Korrin I would like to leave after the Christmas holiday period, so I could get my commission bonuses paid out. She nodded in agreement and said it was a good idea. She told me to play it calm, try not to rock the boat at home, and keep what she was about to tell me in the strictest of confidence—not to even share it with my sister in Florida, any family member, or my girls.

I started writing.

- *Open a savings account at the bank in the mall in your name only and put away a portion of your paycheck every week.*

- *Use the store's address so any correspondence from the bank comes to you at the store.*

- *Open a safe deposit box at the same bank.*

- *Start taking the most important documents from your home and placing them in the safe deposit box: passports, social security cards, medical ID cards, birth certificates, deed to home, bank cards, school ID cards, school report cards, immunization cards, copies of utility bills in my name, resume, high school diploma, prescriptions that needed to be refilled, and any other personal documents. Don't take them all at once; do it gradually.*

- *Make a list of all important numbers and keep them in an address book for reference: family doctors, dentists, opticians, pharmacies.*

- *Keep my writing journal on me at all times. Never leave it out for anyone to access.*

- *Use the computer at work during break time to look into the school district where my sister lives in Florida to be prepared to have Kay transferred. Record the school's number for quick access.*

Once I finished writing, I looked up at Korrin with gratitude. I was so choked up that all I could do was place my right hand over the left side of my chest and let my eyes say the words.

She nodded and said, "I am so happy to help, and I will always be here for you. You don't deserve to be treated this way, and it is time you put yourself and your children first. Thank you for sharing with me."

I got up and walked out of her office, armed with a plan. For the first time in six years, I felt like I had my power back. I went to work, and for the next six hours, I was on top of the world.

I called Mr. that afternoon and told him he did not have to come and get me because I was getting a ride with a coworker. He was okay with that, which was surprising because he never wanted me to invite anyone except for family over to our home. But maybe he was relieved that he did not have to pick me up, and he knew I would not invite my coworker into the house. I was grateful that Laura offered me a ride home that day. I was happy that I did not have to sit in the car with Mr. the evening after such a huge physical fight over two dollars.

I was mostly quiet on the way home, and Laura sensed that I needed that. As I sat in the car deep in thought, rehashing the events of the day, another fear gripped me. I do not own a car. How would I be able to pull off leaving? Once Laura's car made the right turn on Apple Tree Lane, my heart was pounding and my palms were sweating. I was nervous about the fate that awaited me at home. I got out of the car, thanked Laura, and walked to my front door. I opened the door to my house and was greeted by my beautiful girls. They were always excited to see me. Mr. was in the family room watching the O. J. Simpson trial on television. He was obsessed with it. I said hello to him and went upstairs. The girls ran behind me.

"Mommy, Mommy, guess what?" Kay said with excitement. "I found the rest of my lunch money in my backpack. I had forgotten to put it back in my purse, so I can give you back the two dollars you gave me this morning."

I turned to her and whispered, "Baby, I knew you had misplaced it, because you have never lost your money before and even if you did, Mommy would have still given you lunch money today."

I hugged her as the tears welled up in my eyes. "I love you, baby," I said.

I left the girls and walked into my bedroom to change and shower. I tore my clothes off as I entered the bathroom, turned the shower on, and sobbed uncontrollably, hoping that no one could hear me over the running shower. Mr. wanted me to punish my child for losing her lunch money, which she did not lose after all, and all of that created a situation that could have turned deadly. As I cried, I thought, would it ever be possible to repair the broken pieces of my heart?

I thought back to the list of things Korrin told me to start doing. As excited as I was when I was sitting in her office writing the list, would I truly ever be able to leave? Would it ever become a reality? It all seemed so impossible in that moment. How would it all work out?

Despair started to set in, and I felt as if I were being pulled back into that dark place. But I thought about the girls and how excited they were to see me, and I snapped out of it. I showered and went into bed without eating. I heard the garage door open and Mr.'s car engine start. He was leaving for the night again. When the car pulled out of the garage and the door closed, I breathed a sigh of relief. I called the girls to come into my bedroom, and they got into the bed with me. We sat in a circle, and I opened my Bible to Psalms 91. I read each line and had the girls repeat after me. I prayed and asked God for His guidance and deliverance. After I sent the girls to their room for the night, I reached for my journal and started writing the escape plan.

I made a list in order of priority. Establishing the bank account and the safe deposit box were the first things I needed to do, and I planned to do it the next day I went to work. The best thing was that the bank was in the mall, next door to my place of employment. As I wrote the plan, there was a huge black hole that was poking through—one that I did not have an answer to. How do I leave the house without having transportation? I still had a few months to think it through. I had somewhat of a timeline laid out. After the holiday season, commission is usually paid the third weekend of January. I would wait to get that paid out and then leave after. In the meantime, I would ask Korrin to give me her advice about leaving the residence.

As all of this was unfolding, I had started to talk on the phone with my friend Tee from Jamaica, with whom I was recently reconnected. I shared with him that I may be leaving my home for good to go to Florida. He told me he would do whatever he could to help. I mentioned to him that I was having anxiety about it because I did not own a vehicle and had no idea how I would leave the house with the girls. Tee suggested that I rent a car. Why had I not thought about that all along? He kept his promise and sent me several hundred dollars in cash through Western Union to put in the account for the car.

Now that the black hole was cemented, I had my total plan in place. I had to keep calm. I tried to avoid Mr. as much as I could because I felt the weight of the secret, and I did not want him to suspect anything. I also kept all the plans from the girls. I could not mention it for fear of them spilling the tea. I was counting down the days to January, but every time I thought about it, I had an anxiety attack. I turned to my journal to write about how I was feeling. My journal gave me a place to pour out my heart. Some of the pages were stiff, and the ink was watermarked from the tears that I shed as I wrote. But I would always get a sense of relief when I closed the journal.

To my surprise, we had a great Christmas at home that year. Mr. allowed us to put up a tree, with all the gifts around it, and we had a ton of fun. At night—every time Mr. left the house—the girls and I continued to sit in a circle on my bed to recite Psalms 91 and pray. I started feeling hopeful. I continued to take the important papers from the house to the safe deposit box at the bank. Things were falling into place.

Tee kept in touch with me throughout this time to make sure I was not backing out or changing my mind. He knew how vulnerable I was and how scared I was to leave. But he kept encouraging me and reassuring me that I was doing the right thing. I called my sister Fay in Florida and asked her if it was okay for me and the girls to come spend some time with her after the holidays, and she graciously said yes. I did not want to tell her what my full plans were at that time. However, I shared my intentions with my other half-sister Charm. She had come to visit us at one point and spent several weeks at the house. Although Mr. was typically on his best behavior when my family was around, there was one instance in which he got angry about a cup in the sink, and he went off on me. Charm was very upset and addressed Mr. on the spot about the way he spoke to me. I begged her to stop to avoid escalating the situation. From that day, she suspected there was more going on in the home than I was willing to share with her. So, at this time, I felt comfortable letting her in on what I was planning. I did not tell her the whole story or when I was planning to leave but enough to let her know that I was thinking about leaving Mr. She encouraged me to do it.

***

January came around, and things were in place. I had some money in the bank, and all my important papers were in the safe deposit box. I had my job transfer papers ready to go, and my last vacation was pending my move date. The only thing I was waiting on was my commission check, which was due to come to me in another week in the amount of $3,600.

At home, I was walking on eggshells. Every day, I tried to make myself invisible so as to not set Mr. off. I told my girls not to touch the walls, to keep the house clean, and to use the cloth wipes to clean any spots on the wall and the floor so he would not get upset. Our nightly Psalms 91 reading was now memorized. We no longer needed the Bible to say it, and my prayers became more desperate pleas for deliverance. I think Kay knew something was up, but she never asked, and I never shared.

Once I received my commission check, my stomach felt as if it was going to drop out of my body. See, every plan I put in place and every decision to move forward was hung up on me receiving that commission check. Now that I had it in my hands, all I could do was shake. I had to move forward. I had no choice. Korrin had put herself out there to get me the help I was praying for. I couldn't back out now. The transfer process was waiting on my date to Florida, which meant I had to go! I freaked out. I sat against a wall outside the mall and cried. My emotions were all over the place. I was happy, I was scared, I was ready to go but afraid of how. What do I say to the girls? I opened my journal and wrote.

January 20

Dear God,

I am scared. I need you. Thank you for giving me a way out. I am not sure what to do ~~know~~ now. Please, please, please, Lord, help me and the girls to leave. I don't want there to be anymore fights. You see my heart, and you know I can't take it anymore. I want to be free of this kind of life even if it's just for Kaydene. He screamed at her, shook her, and made her pee herself, and I wanted to kill him. But I was afraid to confront him. I did not want another physical altercation, especially in front of them. My heart is so broken for my daughters. Shay loves him, and he loves her, but he treats Kay so different. I want the three of us to be happy together. Help me help me help me help me help me help me help me help me help me please, Lord, please, hear my cry to you. I am afraid, give me the courage, provide a way out. Maybe if he leaves, then we can leave in a rent-a-car. Give your daughter strength, Lord. Maybe I'll rent the car next week, park it down the street, and walk to the house, but tell him that Laura dropped me off. Yes, Lord, thank you for that plan, that's a good one. That's what I am going to do. I love you, Jesus. Amen.

CHAPTER TWELVE

THE ESCAPE

On Thursday, January 26, I went to work like any other day—late—because Mr. refused to take me on time. I was extremely quiet on the drive because this was *the day*. When I got there, I asked Laura if she could drop me off at the car rental office during my lunch break, and she said yes. I rented a car for the weekend, not knowing when or how all this was going to play out. I wanted to give myself a few days to make it happen. I drove the car back to work and completed my shift. Because Laura had taken me a few times, I called Mr. to let him know that she was going to take me home that evening. He was okay with it because he did not have to make that trip to get me.

On my way home in the rental, I was shaking so hard, I had to pull over at a gas station and get a cup of coffee. My entire insides were trembling. I felt sick to my stomach. All kinds of thoughts were going through my mind. Where do I park the car? What if he pulls up as I am coming out of the car? What if my neighbor sees me and wonders why I am parking down the street from my house? How? What if? What's going to happen? These questions kept flashing through my mind as I tried to get ahold of myself. I paid for the coffee and exited the gas station. I sat in the car, took several sips, closed my eyes, and prayed. It was dusk, and the night approaching felt like a blanket slowly covering me from visibility. Nighttime was my favorite time of the day. It covered me and made me invisible. I hid myself in the shadows of the night so that I did not have to deal with anyone looking at me or me looking at myself. But here I was, sitting in a car that I rented, because I finally mustered up the courage to be seen again. I drove home.

I parked the car a few houses down from mine and waited. When it seemed all was quiet and safe, I got out of the car and walked to the house. I opened the front door and went in. My girls ran to greet me, and I hugged them so hard knowing that we may be leaving sometime soon. I picked Shay up and whispered to her that I needed some strength. She hugged me with all her might, and I kissed her on the cheek. Her hugs did give me strength. They reminded me of how she saved our lives, and it made me stronger. Mr. was in the family room watching the O. J. Simpson trial again. I never understood his over-the-top obsession with this trial, but he was glued to the TV when it was on. I said hello and then went upstairs. I showered, changed into my PJs, and went back downstairs to eat.

Later that night, something ticked Mr. off and he started cussing and swearing at me. This time, I argued back. I am not sure if I wanted something to happen between us, so I could have an out to leave that night or if I reacted because of all the built-up resentment and anxiety that I was feeling. I was just tired of taking his crap and not standing up for myself. Knowing that I finally had a way out also gave me some courage. Mr. got all the way up into my face, his eyes filled with rage as he hurled insults at me. One of his eyes closed as the other one became extremely dark. It was an intimidating and scary sight to see. He called me disgusting names and told me how stupid I acted. The girls started crying, and he shouted at them to shut up. His words pierced holes in me. I don't think he ever truly loved me. I was a figment of a woman he wanted, but over the years, I no longer represented that for him. That had to be the reason why it was okay for him to tear me down verbally. No man could truly love a woman and hurt her so deeply with his words. I was crying because I did not want it to get physical with the girls already being so upset, and because I was done. He walked away from me, walked toward the garage, and opened the door. I heard the engine start. He had picked a fight so he had a reason to leave. Was this the opportunity I had been waiting for?

I called for the girls to come to me, and I told them that I wanted to leave Mr. for good. I told them that I had a car parked outside, but I was afraid he would come back while we were trying to leave.

"Mommy, let's go, let's go, please, please, please, let's leave right now," Kay said. "I don't want to stay here anymore. He is mean to you and me. I am unhappy and sad every day. I miss my mommy that used to be in Jamaica. Please don't stay."

My heart sank as my daughter pleaded with me to leave.

I fought the tears as I replied, "But we have nothing packed and I don't know what to do."

Everything felt like it was going in slow motion. What are the odds that he picked a fight with me the same day I rented a car? This had to be a sign from God.

"Mom, don't worry about us," Kay said. "I have been helping you already."

I came to find out that Kay had her plans as well. In the ceiling of her bedroom was a door to the attic with a pull-down string. She would visit the attic frequently when no one was at home. It was her escape place, her secret spot. We all knew that Mr. did not go into the attic, and neither did I, as I hated climbing those stairs. But Kay was not just going to the attic to escape; she had a reason. She knew what was happening between Mr. and me. Kay saw the way he treated me and heard the condescending manner in which he often spoke to me. She did not recognize her mother. Her once-powerful, vibrant, Miss Congeniality mother had become withdrawn and afraid to speak up for herself. So, to take matters into her own hands and to provide a way out for her mom, Kay jumped into action.

She started taking articles of clothing for herself and her sister into the attic and hiding them in black trash bags. She put away shoes, socks, books, toys, and anything she thought would be significant enough, so if I came to my senses and decided to leave, they would already be packed. I kept wondering why their clothes and socks were always missing. The more I bought, it seemed, the more they disappeared. On this night, Kay took me by the hand and walked with me into her bedroom. She pulled down the door to the attic and climbed up. I asked her what she was doing, and before I knew it, she was throwing filled trash bags down to me.

"Mom," she said, "I have been packing for Shay and me for a while, so that when you were ready to leave, you would not have to worry about packing our things. We have everything we need in these six trash bags."

I was shocked.

Climbing down from the attic, she said, "I'll get some more bags and pack your stuff, Mommy, and while I'm doing that, you should write him a letter and leave it for him, so he knows we left."

Oh my god, I thought, from the mouth of babes.

She ran to the kitchen, grabbed more trash bags, and started going through my drawers and closet filling the bags with my things. I was shaking as I wrote the letter to Mr. The actions of my daughter propelled me to snap out of the daze and get going. I ran into the bathroom and got what I needed.

Shay had no clue what was happening; she was just happy that she did not have to be in bed. Kay told her it was an adventure. I pulled my sweater over my PJs, took the car keys out of my purse, and went to get the rental car. I opened the garage door and ran to where it was parked. I drove it into the garage, turned the engine off, and closed the door, so no one would see what was going on. Although it was late, we had nosey neighbors, and I think they knew I was being abused.

I checked the drawers of my dresser to make sure all my underclothes were packed. Kay had packed all she could into four trash bags. She helped me take the ten bags to the garage, and we loaded the car. We ran back into the house, and I placed the letter on the bed. I told the girls to put their coats on and go to the garage as I grabbed my purse. I had no car seat, so I had Shay sit in Kay's lap on the front seat, and I strapped them in together. I opened the garage, turned the car engine on, and pulled out into the driveway. I was shaking so hard and praying he would not come home before his usual time—dawn. Crazy thoughts were running through my mind as I ran back into the garage, closed the door, and then exited the house through the front door. I jumped in the car, pulled out of that driveway, and never looked back. It was around midnight on that cold January night, and as I drove away from Apple Tree Lane, I felt as if the darkness of the night swallowed us up in its blanket. We did it! We escaped. And he never saw it coming. He underestimated the strength of the stupid woman.

I drove for miles in silence as I thought about what was next. I had no clue as to how I was going to navigate our journey to Florida, but we were together, we were free, and that's all that mattered in that moment. I would never leave my girls. We were a package deal, and if it meant that we could only afford one slice of bread, it would be cut in three pieces—one piece for each of us.

I saw the lights of a hotel and pulled in. Shay was sleeping, but Kay was still awake. I left the girls in the car and went to see if there was a room available. I checked in and got the keys. I pulled the car to the closest exit door to my room block. I did not want to be taking trash bags into the hotel through the main entrance. I grabbed all the bags except for the ones in the trunk and took them inside. In the hotel room, I started pacing back and forth, trying to plan the next move. I grabbed my journal, looked at my action list and made some additional notes.

- *Call Korrin to give update (will not be going back to work in NJ)*
- *Pick up current paycheck from work and cash it*
- *Close bank account and empty safe deposit box*
- *Call HR director in Florida and give him vacation time off and start date*
- *Buy three suitcases (do this first)*
- *Purchase three one-way tickets to Florida (maybe leaving from Newark airport?)*

- *Call Tee and my sister Fay to tell them when I'll be arriving*
- *Car rental?? Where do I leave the car? Call rental company to ask if car can be left at airport.*

When I checked the time, it was almost 3 a.m. It was the perfect time to run errands without the fear of being caught. I had to make my moves before dawn. Mr. would not see the note on the bed or realize we were gone until he woke up in the family room and sensed that there was no movement upstairs. I gave myself until 10 a.m. to get everything done before he freaked out and started searching for us. That gave me enough time to get through some of the things on my list. I woke the girls, who were both sleeping, and told them to get changed because we were going shopping. We took a trip to a twenty-four-hour Kmart. I bought three suitcases, a cap for myself, tons of snacks and microwaveable meals, juices, water, travel-size toiletries, books, and a few toys for Shay. When we got back to the hotel, Kay helped me take the rest of the trash bags out of the trunk of the car. After we all had a bite to eat, I turned the television on, lay on the bed with my arms around my girls, and fell asleep.

When I awoke, the television was still on and the time on the news said 8:30 a.m. It took some time for me to get adjusted to my new environment. The reality of the last twenty-four hours hit me, and I jumped out of the bed. I grabbed my journal and looked at my list. I had to call Korrin and let her know that I'd left and would not be coming back to work. I also wanted to warn her that Mr. may show up at the store and that no one should give him any information. I picked up the hotel phone and dialed.

I told Korrin everything, and she offered to call the HR director on my behalf and give him all the updates. Because it was Friday, I knew I needed to get to the bank to take care of what was on my list. I put together breakfast for the girls, woke Kay up and told her what to do, and left for the mall wearing my cap so I would be incognito. I was praying that time was on my side. I had to get everything done and be back to the hotel before 10 a.m. I drove like a crazy woman. When I arrived at the mall, I went to the store and picked up my paycheck from HR. I then went to the bank, took everything from the safe deposit box, cashed my check, pulled all my money out, and closed both the savings account and the safety deposit box account. I walked back to the car with my head lowered and got in and drove away. It was the last time I would ever see Deptford Mall in New Jersey.

When I got back to the hotel room, I breathed a sigh of relief. I made a call to Tee and told him that I left and was at a hotel. He was proud of me. I told him that I wanted to buy three one-way tickets to Fort Lauderdale and asked if he would pick us up. My sister worked on Sundays, so this would save us from having to take a taxi to her house. He said, "Absolutely." I needed someone in my family to know that we were safe in case Mr. decided to reach out to them to say we were missing. I called my sister Charm and told her that I'd left and if he called her to pretend she knew nothing.

Around noon, the hotel phone rang, It was Korrin. She gave me the update on my transfer. It was all set. I could take the first week of February as vacation time to get settled in Florida, and my start date at Aventura would be February 7. Then, she said that Mr. came to the store looking for me and created a scene. He accused them of knowing where I was and threatened to call the FBI to let them know that I had kidnapped his daughter. They alerted security at the store and asked him to leave. Korrin said she would mention it to the Florida team as well, so they would look out for my safety. I knew in my heart it was getting dangerously close for comfort. I was still in New Jersey, and Mr. was out searching for me. I had to act fast. I called a travel agency and reserved three one-way tickets to Florida for the coming Sunday. I had twenty-four hours to get to the travel agency and pay for the tickets to get them in hand. I had to be strategic in everything I was doing at this point. I called Tee and Fay to let them know that I would be arriving on Sunday. I told Fay that Tee would pick me up from the airport and I would see her at the house.

In the meantime, Shay was getting fussy. She wanted her dad and her refrigerator. She had a habit of opening the refrigerator every morning and climbing in it. I just always thought of it as her being a little adventurous baby girl. Kay told her there would be no more climbing in the refrigerator and that we were on another adventure and taking a trip on an airplane. Kay calmed her down, taking that pressure off my hands. Because it was daylight and I was afraid to leave for the travel agency, I decided to transfer the items from the trash bags into the suitcases and wait until it became dark to go pick up the tickets. I reached out to my sister Charm who told me that Mr. had called her crying and asked if she knew that I had left, She acted very surprised and told him no. He told her that he knew my job had something to do with it, but they refused to give him any information. That reassured me that he had no clue where I was.

I got to the travel agency later that evening and paid for the three tickets. We stayed in for the rest of the night, ordered dinner in, and sat on the hotel bed. The next day was Saturday, and we spent the day taking the rest of the items from the trash bags and putting them in the suitcases.

Bright and early Sunday morning, we got dressed, placed the suitcases in the car, checked out of the hotel, and drove to Newark airport. We dropped the car off at the rental car return, got on the shuttle to the airport, and boarded the nonstop flight to Fort Lauderdale. We were finally free. I whispered a prayer and thanked God for my life, my girls, Korrin, and my job.

CHAPTER THIRTEEN

INTO THE FIRE

Tee kept his promise and picked us up from the airport. It was great to see him. He was surprised at how much Kay had grown. He had known her when she was a toddler. He looked at me from head to toe and walked around me as if he was sizing me up. He said I looked thinner than he remembered, and all I could do was chuckle. He had not changed a bit.

Tee drove us to my sister's home. I was so happy to see my nephews, my sister, and my brother-in-law, and they were happy to see us. I mentioned to my sister that I would not be going back and shared with her what I had been experiencing with Mr. She was happy that I'd left, although she was a little upset that I never shared what I was experiencing with her. I assured her that I transferred with my company and that I had guaranteed employment. I just needed a place to stay temporarily until I got on my feet. I told her I would not be with her for too long. She had a husband and three sons in her small three-bedroom home, but she opened her arms and accommodated us. She shifted things around to make us as comfortable as she could. My oldest nephew was getting ready to go to the Marines, so she had the middle son share the bedroom with his older brother. We would share the room with her youngest son. That bedroom had a bunk bed. The bottom bunk was a full-sized bed, and the top was a twin. For the next six months, my girls and I slept on the bottom bunk and lived out of our suitcases. My youngest nephew slept on the top bunk. It was not easy, but we made it work.

The first order of business was to get a car. I found a used Toyota Corolla with a ridiculous interest rate, but it was a necessity. I got the car and was happy that I had some type of independence. I enrolled the girls in school. Kay went to the middle school and Shay to the preschool down the street, within walking distance from my sister's home. I called the HR director to let him know that I would be at work on February 7.

That Monday morning when I went to Aventura, I met the director face to face. I thanked him for his help and told him if I had not been guaranteed a job, I would still be in New Jersey living with the abuse. The only department with an opening was the men's shoe department. I was introduced to the department manager, Tom, who was absolutely amazing. My rate was $7.50 per hour plus commission. I could make as much as possible if I sold as much as possible. Tom showed me around and trained me on how to sell men's shoes. I hated it! But I had no choice. Knowing that I could transfer to another department or move up in the store gave me hope that I could grow within the company. I was grateful despite it all.

The Aventura store got word from the New Jersey store that Mr. was threatening to come to Florida. I have no idea how he found out where I was. The store security was alerted every shift I worked and had me on camera for safety purposes. I am forever thankful for this amazing company, and the way they advocated on my behalf. My sister Fay also had communication with Mr., and she told him in no uncertain terms that he would never be able to hurt me or my girls again.

We settled in at my sister's as best we could under the circumstances. One day, I got a call from Shay's preschool. They had some concerns and wanted me to meet with a counselor and child care specialist at our home. I was very uneasy. I told Fay and asked if she would be willing to sit with me in the meeting. The meeting was confirmed, and they came to my sister's house. The counselor took a sheet of paper from her bag that was folded in half. She unfolded the paper and showed it to my sister and me. She proceeded to say what was on the paper was concerning to them and they needed to find out what is happening at home. During art time at preschool, Shay, at only four years old, drew a picture of two stick figures: one was a man and the other was a woman. The man had his arm outstretched and was punching the woman in her face. They told me that it was the same thing she drew every day. When I saw the paper with the images, I broke down. I had no idea Shay, a baby, could recall what she saw and translate it to paper in that manner. I felt vulnerable and ashamed.

My sister shared with the counselor and the child care specialist what we had been through. They praised me for my courage to leave and assured me that they would keep their eye on Shay to make sure she was okay. I thanked them, and they left. My sister held my hands and prayed for me.

I was afraid to go to work sometimes for the fear that, one day, Mr. might show up. I was happy to have a job that had benefits so I could take care of my girls, but I struggled at working hard enough to make my commissions. My sister encouraged me to get certified to become a home health aid, like her, because there was a lot of money in that field. I did enroll to get certified but refused to leave my job because of how they continued to assist me. I never wanted to give up something that was guaranteed for something that was uncertain at that time. She thought I was stubborn.

My girls were always left in the care of my sister and her family when I was away at work. I came home earlier than usual from work one day and saw Kay playing with my brother-in-law in the bedroom he shared with my sister. She was sitting on his back, and he had no shirt on. When I asked what was going on, she told me that he asked her to burst the pimples on his back. He must have seen the look of *what the hell?* on my face because he said to me, "It's no big deal, Sis."

My heart sank. I demanded that Kay get up and leave the room. Everything about that sight was concerning to me. It dawned on me that when my sister and I were at work, my girls were left in the care of my brother-in-law (if he got home before us) and my nephews. I felt extremely uncomfortable for the first time since we moved in with them, and I knew that the time had come for me to leave that space.

I called Tee and asked him for his help to find a place. He took me around, and we found a one-bedroom apartment. He gave me the down payment to secure the unit. Knowing that we had no furniture except for three suitcases, he took me furniture shopping. The furniture store had a deal where we would not have to pay the monthly payment for two years. We bought a queen bedroom set, living room furniture, and a television.

The girls and I moved into the new apartment six months after we ran away to Florida. We loved it. We were ecstatic to have our own place. We hung our clothes in the closet, which was a big deal for us. Living out of our suitcases for six months was very difficult. In the new place, we still slept together in the same bed, but we had much more space. Money was tight, but Kay made a food list every week to make sure we stayed on budget of twenty dollars a week for meals. I marveled at how smart she was at eleven years old.

During the summertime, when the girls were out of school, Kay babysat Shay when I was at work. Because I was leaving them alone on a daily basis, we established a special code for answering the telephone and the door. They were not to answer the phone or open the door unless they recognized the special code.

Tee kept coming by the new apartment trying to get with me, but I was not in a good place mentally and I did not want to get involved while I was in that space. I did not want to bring that into the home with my girls. It was way too soon. I was happy being in the friend zone with him, especially because he lived with his significant other. Tee and I kept our relationship as great friends, and that was the extent. He had helped me tremendously, and I was grateful for his kindness. Every once in a while, he would invite me out for lunch or dinner to his friend's restaurant. It was the best Jamaican restaurant in Florida, according to Tee, and he always supported the owner due to their friendship. I had the opportunity to meet the owner a few times while I was at the restaurant, and he was a truly awesome guy with a great family.

I knew my full-time job would not meet the needs of my living expenses, so I applied for a job at a supermarket to help supplement my income. I also asked my sister if I could work with her patients on the Sabbath (Friday through Saturday) while she went to church. It was draining. I had three jobs, but it was still hard to pay for our necessities. The rent was $650 per month, and my car payment was $400. Factor in car insurance, utilities, and food, and I was always robbing Peter to pay Paul. My total salary did not cover the total bills. My car stopped one day in the middle of the highway because the alternator was shot. I had to get it towed to a shop and pay for the repairs, which put me so behind with the bills that I missed a rent payment.

While my car was in the shop, I took public transportation to work. One day on my way home from work, I stopped to pick up a few items from the grocery store before taking the bus home. The items were in two paper bags. When the bus got to my stop, it was pouring so hard and I did not have an umbrella. When the bus driver opened the door, I picked up my bags and hesitated to get off the bus because I knew the rain would rip the paper bags apart.

The bus driver said, "Ma'am, you have to get off. I can't wait for the rain to stop because I am on a schedule."

I got off the bus holding onto my paper bags filled with the items I bought to feed us for the week. I tried to put them under my arms to prevent them from getting wet. The bus stop was a short distance from my apartment complex, but the rain was too heavy for my body to cover the bags, and they fell apart. My groceries scattered all across the sidewalk. The eggs were broken, and the tomatoes and onions were being washed away by all the water. I stood in the rain and screamed, losing total control of my emotions. Cars were driving by at high speeds, and when they hit the puddles, I was sprayed from head to toe.

I looked up to the sky and said, "Why, God, why? What's next? I am trying, but I am failing."

After what seemed like an eternity, I picked up the bread, the chicken, and the bag with the rice and walked to my apartment sobbing.

When I opened the apartment door, I fell to the floor. I felt like the walls were closing in on me. I was struggling to keep it all together. Kay took what I had in my hands to the kitchen, and Shay started crying because she saw how wet and upset I was. I told them what had happened.

"It's okay, Mommy," Kay said. "You just have to be strong."

She became the strongest force in my life during that time, while Shay continued to give me strength through her hugs. After I calmed down, I took a shower, made dinner, and retired for the evening.

My sister Shelly came to visit me the following week. I was happy to have her around. She always made me feel better. I did not have enough money to get my car out of the shop, plus pay the installment for that month, and I was fifteen days behind in the rent. I only had a portion of the rent, but the leasing office would not take the partial payment. I poured my heart out to my sister, and immediately, she jumped into action. She got on the phone and started calling friends to see if they could help her help me. One friend agreed to give us $400 to pay the car loan, and I used my paycheck to pay for the repairs. I was happy to get my car back, but now I was in a deeper hole with the rent. By the time I was able to pay the rent that was in arrears, I was already behind for the current month's rent. I could not get a break. I got a warning notice on my door that said I was thirty days behind in the rent. If I did not bring my account current, they would be taking legal action. But I chose to make the car note, car insurance, utility bills, and our food the priorities. Thirty days later, I get another notice. I was now two months behind with the rent, and if I did not pay up in fourteen days, I would be evicted.

Just seeing that word—*evicted*—on paper sent chills up my spine. I knew I could not go back to my sister's house because of how strange things were right before we left. I was also embarrassed to keep asking people for help. I shivered at having to go into a shelter or live in my car. I drove to a phone booth and made a call to Mr. to ask him to take us back! I felt like I took my kids out of the frying pan and threw them in the fire. At least we had a roof over our head when we lived with him. I did not care about myself or if he continued to abuse me. I just wanted a home for my kids. In that moment, I regretted leaving.

When Mr. answered the phone and I told him what I wanted to do, his exact words were, "I have moved on with my life. You need to move on too."

I hung up the phone and broke down. A flood of emotions took over. I felt so confused. On the one hand, I was relieved at his response because I knew he had given up looking for us and did not care what happened, but on the other hand, it confirmed that I might become homeless.

When I told the girls that I had asked to go back, Kay cried and said, "Mommy, we can't. I will do everything to help you. Please don't go back to him."

After hearing her words, I silently thanked God that Mr. responded the way he did for her sake. In my weak moment, I was willing to go backwards after it took me so long to leave. I was weak and stupid. Maybe Mr. had been right about me all along.

CHAPTER FOURTEEN

A CLOSE CALL

We were evicted with no place to go. I had no choice but to call my brother-in-law, as the complex was getting ready to throw my furniture out into the courtyard of the building. He came and placed our furniture in his truck. The reality of homelessness hit me like a ton of bricks, and I completely shut down. I refused to talk. I was trying to be strong for my girls, but I could not find the will. My girls carried me with their laughter and love. They did everything in their power to not be needy. Kay was my rock, and I leaned on her. It was so unfair because she was a baby tossed into a world of chaos. That would haunt me for years to come. Both my sisters decided to help me figure out my situation. Fay said she had a friend who owned a restaurant and she was going to ask him for help. Shelly was on the phone talking to her friends, too.

Fay drove us downtown to see her friend, who she was going to ask for the money. Come to find out, it was Tee's friend who owned the restaurant. What a coincidence and embarrassment. My sister told him our story, and he was overcome with compassion. He loaned my sister $1,000 to give to me. He walked out of the restaurant with her, so he could meet me face to face and was surprised to see that it was me. I thanked him and promised to pay him back in installments. He told me not to worry about it at that time, but to try and find a place so we would not have to be on the streets. That night, the kids and I stayed at a motel. The next day, we drove around trying to find a place with a For Rent sign. After what seemed like hours, we found a move-in-ready duplex. We had to pay $900 to get it: one month's rent and a $300 deposit. I had $100 left in my pocket. We moved in, and I bought groceries with the money I had left over. My brother-in-law delivered my furniture, and I did not have to worry about being on the streets—at least not for the next month.

My sister Shelly and I spoke to our mom, who was in New York at the time. After hearing what I had been going through, she suggested that she come down to help with the girls so that I would not have to worry about them. I was so excited to have my mom with me. She was a breath of fresh air, and Kay had always been her baby. In hindsight, I think that Mom offered to come mostly for Kay's sake.

My sister Fay called to say that Earl, the restaurant owner who loaned us the money, wanted to check on me and the girls. She asked if she could give him my address. Knowing that he loaned me so much money and I was a stranger, I felt obligated to say yes. He stopped by to see us a few days later. When he walked in our home, he noticed that Mom was sitting on the couch and the girls were sitting on the floor eating. I introduced him to them. It was awkward having him in my place, but he was the reason we had it. He walked around my apartment, said his goodbyes, and then asked if I would step outside with him. I closed the door behind me. He turned to me and said that he noticed we did not have a dining table or any bed in the second bedroom and he wanted to help me purchase those. I was shocked. I told him that I already owed him and didn't know when I would be able to pay him back, so I could not take another loan. He said this one was a gift. He gave me another $1,000 and suggested that I buy a bed for my mom to sleep on and a dining table. He left, and when I told my mom, she said that God was looking out for me. I bought the furniture and put the balance of the money in the bank so I could pay the next month's rent.

In the meantime, things were picking up at work. I got promoted to an assistant sales manager, which gave me an increase in pay. I was no longer on commission and was now making $10 an hour. I quit my job at the grocery store. I started to feel as if things were turning around for me.

Earl kept calling me to check in and often asked me about Tee. He knew that Tee and I had dated in Jamaica and that we were friends. He said Tee talked about me a lot. Earl was a married man with a sweet wife and two teenage children, so I never suspected he had an interest in me until that Thanksgiving Day. My sister Fay invited all of us for dinner at her house, and she thought it would be great to invite Earl as a thank you for his generosity. He came when we were almost done eating. He said hello and had some pie. When he was getting ready to leave, he asked me to walk outside with him. He invited me out to a Dennis Brown concert. I loved Dennis Brown, but I felt a little uneasy saying yes and ungrateful saying no. I was caught between a rock and a hard place. Why would a married man want to invite me out to a concert? But after thinking back to all he had done for me and my kids, I felt indebted to go. Reluctantly, I said yes.

When Earl picked me up for the concert, he looked and smelled great. The event was super awesome. It was the first time since running away to Florida that I truly felt as if I could let my hair down and have some fun. No one knew me there, and it was mostly dark, so I had no fear that this would get back to his wife. This was a one-and-done thing, I told myself, and I would never accept another invitation from him.

I was enjoying the music. Earl asked if I wanted a drink, and he left to get it for me. As I was standing there waiting, moving to the beat of D. Brown's lyrics, I felt a presence behind me. I recognized the fragrance and knew it was him. Before I could turn around to take my drink, he placed his lips in the contour of my neck and gently kissed me. I felt a tingle run all through my body, down to my toes. This cannot happen, I thought. Not good, Joan, not good. He then put his arms around my waist and held me ever so close to him. I was lost in the tenderness of his touch. I relaxed my body and laid my head back in his comfort. After years of coldness from Mr., my body was loving the warmth of Earl's embrace. The drink did not help either. It made me forget about everything that was morally right.

On our way home from the concert, he asked if I wanted to stay at a hotel with him. I said absolutely not and told him I was offended that he asked me to. He apologized profusely and took me home.

A few months passed without hearing much from Earl, until he called to say it was important that he saw me so we could talk. He came by and picked me up one evening, and we went for a drive. He shared how much he felt bad that he offended me and that he was very sorry. He told me that he had fallen in love with my girls and my mom and he wanted to be in my life to make sure I was okay. He wanted to be my friend because he loved being around me. I told him I would love to just be friends with him and I promised to pay him back. We started spending a lot of time together, becoming close friends. But eventually, I let my guard down too much. One thing led to another, and we got intimately involved.

CHAPTER FIFTEEN

A SIGNIFICANT LOSS

Having my mom around made all the difference in the world. She cooked breakfast and dinner for us every day, and I never had to worry about anything. I was finally able to tell her all about my experience with Mr.—all the things I had hid before I had the opportunity to open up and share with her. She told me that she knew something was wrong that day he threw the water on me in front of her. Only a man who had no respect for his wife would behave that way in front of his wife's mother. That also meant that he had no respect for her either. She said she had been worried for me and Kay every day after that incident.

I also told her about Earl and everything that had happened between us. My mother was a quiet, nonjudgmental woman, and God knew that was what I needed at that time. I was way too fragile to have judgment passed on me. She never gave me a lecture about Earl; instead, she held me and told me that everything would be okay. I felt like a burden lifted off me once I told her everything. She was my rock. But we'd soon find out she had her own reasons for worry.

Mom had been having pains in her stomach to the point where she was unable to sleep. When we took her to see a doctor, her diagnosis resulted in her needing to have a major surgery. I was happy when she got relief from all the pain, though it was a difficult healing process. At one point, her incision busted open and I had to rush her back to the surgeon's office. The doctor showed me how to clean the wound and use Steri strips to close it back together. I did that daily for several weeks until it finally healed.

One day, I noticed that something was different about her. She was washing the dishes and signing a hymn I grew up hearing:

Pass me not, O gentle Savior,
hear my humble cry;
while on others thou art calling, do not pass me by.
Savior, Savior,
hear my humble cry;
while on others thou art calling,
do not pass me by.

She sang those lyrics over and over again, and she was crying. I had a sinking feeling in my heart. I knew how much she had suffered in life. I knew the devastating betrayal she had experienced. I knew her life story intimately, and it was one filled with many adversities. I knew her dreams and her goals, and I also knew she was never able to achieve them. However, she settled with the joy of accepting her children as her greatest accomplishments. Promises that were made to her by my dad, the man she had loved for a lifetime, were broken. As I listened to her and saw the tears, my heart knew her pain. Her pain was also my pain because I knew her story of love and loss. I loved her deeply and wanted to make her proud of me. I wanted to give her what she never had—a home to call her own—but I was not in the position at the time to do that. That made me cry.

A few weeks later, I planned a July 4th cookout and invited friends and family to come over. I wanted Mom to have some fun. My dad and mom were no longer in a relationship as husband and wife, but they had formed a cordial friendship. It was vital for them to maintain some ties for the sake of their children and grandchildren. So I invited my dad and my aunt, who had come up to visit from Jamaica, to the cookout. It was an amazing time of food, fun, and laughter.

After everything was over, Mom told me that she was having pains in her throat and that it felt as if her food was stuck there. I tried giving her something hot to drink, but that would not go down either. I took her to the emergency room.

I stayed outside in the waiting room as the doctors took her back to be seen. It seemed like forever before someone came out to talk to me. The doctor told me that food was lodged in her throat and esophagus, and they had to use a tube to get it out. He went on to say that upon further tests of her digestive system, they saw what appeared to be tumors. They did not know the extent of what was happening or what type of tumors they were, but they were going to do an emergency exploratory surgery to get to the bottom of it. They were getting ready to do the surgery and they would come back to give me the update when it was over. I kept asking how and why, but they were not able to give me a definite answer until the surgery was performed and the biopsy results came back. The word *biopsy* always scared me. I started panicking. It was around 4 a.m. in the morning, and I did not know what to do or who to call. I paced back and forth in the hospital and, at one point, sat down and fell asleep.

When the doctor finally came out of surgery, he told me that my mom was in the ICU.

"What is her diagnosis?" I asked.

"Your mom has stage 4 esophageal cancer," he said. "The cancer is in her throat, esophagus, digestive system, stomach, and intestines."

Everything started spinning, and I could no longer comprehend anything he was saying. I let out a wail and dropped to the floor. I was shattered.

Once I got ahold of myself, I asked to see her.

There were tubes everywhere, and she had a colostomy bag. As I was rubbing her hand, she opened her eyes. I asked her if she knew what was happening, and she nodded her head yes. My heart broke into a million pieces.

"I'm sorry you have to go through this," I cried.

She shook her head. "Don't cry."

I thought back to that day she was singing and crying in the kitchen. In my heart, I knew she suspected she was ill.

I called my sister Fay and told her what was happening. Then I called my brothers and sister in New York. Fay brought my dad and aunt to the hospital. This was such a big blow to all of us. The doctors spoke with my mom and the family and told us what the options were. Chemo was not an option at the final stage. The doctors said there was nothing they could do to heal her. Mom chose hospice. She did not want to be on any life support as she did not want to be a burden to her children.

A week later, she was transferred to hospice care. It was all so surreal. I took the girls to see her every day. She was never alone; there was always someone visiting her.

Everyone who knew Ena Rebecca Hibbert-Thaxter knew how gentle and kind she was. She was a simple, shy, reserved, and introverted woman who loved beyond limits. She never got to attend school past the sixth grade, but she was brilliant, self-taught. She was an avid reader and studied history and geography on her own, becoming an expert. Her favorite sports were boxing and cricket, and she could tell you everything about the greats in those sports. She was also a movie buff and loved Cary Grant and Charlton Heston, who won awards for films like *Ben Hur* and *The Ten Commandments*. I grew up with that type of influence from a mother who was never given the opportunity to be as great as she could have been. But her essence was planted in the DNA of her children, and that was our legacy.

I saw the first signs of the deteriorative effects of cancer while she was in hospice. My birthday was fast approaching, and I was praying to God to not let her pass on that day. The eve of my birthday came around, and I spent most of the day with her. Around 1 a.m. when she fell asleep, I left to go home and get some rest, so I could be back when she woke up.

On my thirty-second birthday, I was awakened at 5 a.m. to my home phone ringing. When I answered, it was the hospice nurse. She told me my mom had woken up soon after I left and asked for me. The nurse said my mom fell into a trance-like state with her eyes halfway open and I should get there as soon as I could. I jumped up, got dressed, and rushed to the hospice.

I sat at my mom's bedside and held her hands.

"Hey, Mama, I am here and it's my birthday. Are you gonna tell me happy birthday?"

She opened her eyes and smiled at me. She pulled on my hand and motioned for me to get closer to her. She was trying to raise her head as if to whisper to me.

I lowered myself and got closer to her and said, "Are you going to say happy birthday?"

She was trying so hard to move her lips as if to say the words, but instead a tear ran down the right side of her face. I leaned in closer and wiped the tear with my hand.

She opened her mouth to say something, but instead she coughed twice. Then I felt her hands go limp.

"Mama? Mama?"

Nothing.

I screamed for the nurse, who ran into the room. She checked her pulse and her heart and pronounced my beautiful mom dead. She was gone. She was sixty-two years old, and she took her flight up to heaven on the same date that she gave birth to me: July 23. It was a devastating loss for me. I fell to the floor in a fetal position and wailed. It could not get any worse.

"Why me, Lord, why me? Not again!" I screamed.

I felt as if I could never get a break. It was one hurdle after the other, one setback after the other—and now, the death of my beloved mom.

A nurse came to get me off the floor and told me that my mom had left her with something for me. The nurse handed me an envelope. In it was a birthday card and a small scroll with a birthday message. In the card, my mom had had someone write, "To my daughter, Joan." In her own handwriting, which was more like a scribble, she wrote "Love, Mom!"

To know she was thinking about my birthday while she was in her last days filled me with deep emotions. I could not stop the tears. I felt so close to her spirit in that moment. I went over to the bed where she lay and held on to her hand until it became cold. I was her first daughter. How significant was it for her to go back to heaven on that day? It was a special moment for me. She waited to see me before she took her last breath, and no one was there but her and me. The nurse said there was one more thing in the envelope. When I looked again, it was my mom's wedding band. She had told them that was the gift she wanted me to have. I lost it again and sobbed. The only finger that her ring could fit on was my right thumb. I put the ring on and never took it off. I promised her that I would wear it for the rest of my life on Earth. I sat in the room with her until they came to take her body.

My mom had a royal send off. The ceremony was packed with friends and family from near and far. My sister Fay, who is actually my paternal half-sister and oldest child on my dad's side, was also there. The law enforcement motorcade was fit for a queen. Mom was blessed with two biological daughters. I am the first and oldest girl, and my sister Shelly is the youngest. Shelly was born on Mom's birthday, and Mom died on my birthday. What profound significance that is!

PART III

PERSEVERANCE

CHAPTER SIXTEEN

FIGHTING AGAINST THE ODDS

My mom's passing rocked the foundation of our family. My sister Shelly was devastated because she was in New York when Mom died and never got to say goodbye properly. My brother Howard used to call Mom his favorite girl, and now there was a void in his life. My dad also took it hard. They had been in each other's lives for more than thirty-five years, and the finality of her death weighed heavily on him. I sometimes wondered if he felt any guilt. Mom was Kay's guardian when I left her in Jamaica, and their bond was special. Kay loved her more than words could express, and although she was only twelve years old, she understood that her grandmother was forever gone, and she was heartbroken. My aunt (my dad's sister), who was Mom's best friend, completely lost it.

I felt as if the weight of the world was on my shoulders. I never truly got a chance to mourn her because I had the responsibility of planning her funeral service. It was tough because she did not have life insurance or a savings account with any money to cover the expenses. My brothers, sisters, and I came up with an action plan and solicited the help of family and friends.

Earl stayed in my corner during that difficult period. He provided financial and emotional support as best he could for me and the girls. He paid a portion of our rent each month so I could stay afloat. Now that my mom was gone, I was back in the predicament of having to leave the girls alone when I was at work. One day, someone gave me some counterfeit bills. He told me he was able to pass it off at various places without anyone suspecting they were fake. I had the bright idea to mix it in with the real money to pay my rent. The landlord traced it back to me and gave me a two-week notice to vacate. Although I told her I had no idea that it was counterfeit, she wanted me gone.

Here we go again. A stupid act that jeopardized our home.

Earl had a friend who was renting one half of his residence. He negotiated a deal with him so we could live there, and we moved in. It was much farther from the girls' schools, so we had to be up super early to get to school and work on time. They did not like that, but we had no choice.

I sat back and analyzed my life. I had not written in my journal since I had escaped New Jersey, so I picked it up and started writing.

On the left side of the page, I wrote, "My current space Q," and on the right side of the page, I wrote, "My intended space A." The left page had the things I wrote about my current life and the *questions* that haunted me. The right side of the page were the intended *answers* to the questions on the left page.

My current space Q

- *What have I done with my life so far?*

- *What have I accomplished?*

- *The decisions I have made have had some adverse consequences on my life! How do I fix that?*

- *Mom lived her life with integrity and decency, and yet, she passed away with her dreams buried inside of her. She left her children to carry on her essence as a woman of substance. But we struggled to find the money to bury her. How could we have prevented that?*

- *It seems as if we have a curse hanging over our heads! How do we break it?*

- *Everywhere I turn, I run into roadblocks. Why? What am I doing wrong?*

- *I would never want my kids faced with this situation if I passed away. What's the fix?*

- *What do I do to change the narrative of my life?*

- *What is the lesson that my life is teaching me?*

- *How do I heal, forgive, and love myself?*

- *Why did Mom have to die?*

My intended space A

This was left blank. I had no answers. That is when I totally lost it. I felt the pain of my mom's absence deep down in my belly. I screamed until I was hoarse. I lay on the floor and sobbed. What had been bottled up inside of me since her funeral finally came out.

There was nothing to write on the right side of the page because I did not have the answers. The fact that I wrote it made me feel better because I was digging deep, trying to find the root cause for my situation. As much as I was still in mourning, Mom's death awakened something inside of me that made me stop and think about the legacy I would leave for my girls. I had to *make the choice* to put a plan in place to *evoke the change*. I was confident that one day I would write the answers to the questions on the left page. I experienced a renewed mindset—a shift—and I was determined to stand and fight to find the answers.

My sister Shelly came to visit us in the new place. We always had fun when we were together, no matter what life threw at us. I love her oh so much. We had a deep conversation about our life and how hard it had been for us since we both left Jamaica. We talked about Mom, how much we missed her, and what her death meant to us.

Shortly after our conversation, I made my way into the kitchen to do the dishes. Out of nowhere, the roof fell onto my head. We had only been at this residence for a few months. When I looked up, there was a hole in the kitchen ceiling, and I could see where the wood had rotted from water damage. The sky was now showing through the ceiling. I was in a state of shock. My sister ran to me to make sure I was not hurt or bleeding. I think the surprise of it all placed me in a state of hysteria where I did not feel any pain. I walked out of the kitchen and I was done. I called Earl to let him know, and he called the owner. They sent someone over to repair it, but I was ready to move on from there. It all seemed like an omen. I could not get a break at all.

And if things could not get any worse, I had a car accident four weeks later, totaling my Toyota Corolla. I sustained minor injuries and burns on my forearms from the airbags, but I was okay otherwise. The driver of the other car took full responsibility, but my car was irreparable. How does someone survive a life like this? Everywhere I turned, I was being persecuted.

Earl loaned me his car to drive until I could get another car. A friend of his wife saw me driving the car and told her that I was having an affair with her husband. Earl told me that his wife had asked him about the affair, but he denied it. He refused to give me details of what was going on at his home with his wife, no matter how much I asked him. So I left it alone. Earl never left my side. I continued to drive his car to work every day for about two months until he went to CarMax one day and bought me a car, putting it in both of our names.

Although everything around me was falling apart, I was excelling at my job. I constructed another Joan outside of my personal existence. When I showed up for work every day, I was my best. I pretended that nothing was going wrong at home. . I was dedicated, I worked extremely hard, and it paid off. I started getting recognized at work for the contribution and impact I was making. It gave me the motivation to work that much harder. I accepted the fact that I was smart and more than enough. Work gave me the platform to be the best in my career.

I found out about a new store opening in South Miami. A position was opening that would give me an opportunity for a big promotion. This would mean the world to me. It was far away from where I was currently living, and I would have to transfer the girls to yet another new school, but it would be a great move for us. I landed the job and moved from the house with the broken roof to a beautiful three-bedroom apartment in Cutler Ridge, South Florida. The promotion doubled my salary, and I was finally able to give my girls a better life.

Something changed in me when I started my new job. I was no longer at the store where security had to watch me on camera every day to make sure no one tried to hurt me. I was no longer in the city where I was evicted, became homeless, lost my mother, had a roof fall on my head, and totaled my car. I left that all behind me. I was given a chance to make things right.

I had a desire to show my mom that the dreams I had as a child were still in my heart, even though years had passed and life had given me nothing but lemons. I revisited my journal and promised myself I was going to create the answers to my questions as opposed to trying to find them. I realized that all the answers were within me.

CHAPTER SEVENTEEN

FOR THE LOVE OF MY DAUGHTER

I approached my new job like a boss. I was the department sales manager for the men's department. My staff and supervisors were amazing, as well as the executive leadership team. I was happy that I never gave up my job. I stuck with it, and I was a product of hard work and dedication. The girls and I loved our new place. We went from sleeping on a full-size bunk bed and living out of our suitcases to having our own rooms and walk-in closets. It seemed that we were finally turning the corner. I had become much more independent and was able to handle my financial responsibilities on my own. But I had the highest level of respect, love, and admiration for Earl. He had found a wounded bird and provided her support and a safety net. He gently cared for, nurtured, and loved her back to independence. Yes, we got involved, and one could sit and pass judgment about our moral indiscretion, but we were both in a space where there was a yearning for friendship, understanding, affection, and love. We were that for each other.

The girls were adjusting in the new school, but I sensed a distance in Kay. She became confrontational with me and had the "mean girl" demeanor with Shay. Life had not been easy for her after leaving Jamaica, but she was my right hand. I leaned on her a lot. Too much. She was still a child but had to quickly adjust to support her mom. That was not the way it was supposed to be. The girls were my everything. I overcame the odds that were stacked against me because they would not let me fail. They each had a specific purpose and role in life by design. Only God could have made it so.

Kay started hanging out with a group of Hispanic kids. I truly did not mind that. I was happy that she had found friends her age to hang out with because she was always with her sister, who was six years younger. The problem was that she was trying too hard to become someone else. She told them she was from the Dominican Republic as a way to fit in, and she was speaking Spanish and emulating their dialect. I am sure she wanted to create a new story about her life. After all, she was a teenager who just wanted to feel like her life was normal instead of the rough roller-coaster existence she had because of the decisions her mother made. But as it stood in the moment, all I knew was that my gifted daughter was not completing her schoolwork or participating in class. I was getting less-than-stellar reports from her teachers, and they were always the same: Kay was not working to her potential, and her grades were slipping. We started butting heads. I was worried about her because I felt as if I could not get through to her. I was afraid I would lose her to an environment in which she had to become someone else to fit in.

Then came another blow. One quiet Saturday evening after dinner and some television, we said our goodnights, and the girls and I went to our separate rooms for bed. About an hour later, Shay came to my room and said that Kay was gone. She told me that she went in her room to say another goodnight, and when she tried to hug her, there were only clothes under the covers. My heart sank, and my stomach cramped. I got up to check Kay's room.

It was around midnight, and Kay was not in her bed. We lived on the first floor of the apartments, and at first, I was terrified that maybe she was kidnapped. But I knew that there was a lock on the window inside that prevented anyone from entering unless they broke the window, and the window was not broken. When I checked the lock, it was obvious that she had gone through it because it was unlocked from the inside. It was also positioned in a way that she could reenter her bedroom from the outside. I knew at that moment that she had left on her own or at the influence of someone else. My heart was pounding. I panicked. With all that was going on with her, I thought she might have run away. I checked her closet and drawers, and everything was still there. I felt a wave of guilt wash over me. I started questioning myself. Was I working too much? I was at work all the time, and she was left to babysit her sister. Even though I could see she had changed, I never dreamed she would sneak out of the house. How had I missed the signs? Or had I just ignored them? The latter was more accurate. I started asking Shay a million questions.

"Do you know who she may be with or if she's been hanging out with anyone different?"

"She has a boyfriend named Angel," Shay said, "and they are always together. When you work late at night, she hangs out at the pool, and then she comes home when she knows you will be home."

I felt nauseous. "Kay has a boyfriend?" I asked.

Shay nodded her head.

She is only fourteen, I thought. She is not even mature enough to have a boyfriend.

"So she leaves you alone in the apartment when she is with Angel?".

Shay nodded again.

I was devastated. What if something happened to Shay while Kay was out with this Angel character? Who is he? I had never even heard that name. Here I was, working extremely hard to make things better for us to provide a life of stability after all our suffering and hardships, and this was the result.

My mind took me all the way back to Kay's dad and me. I was also fourteen when I met Tony, and I felt as if I knew everything then.

"Mom, let's go look for her," Shay said. "I know the places that she hangs out sometimes."

We left the apartment around 12:30 a.m. to look for my child. We searched the pool area, the courtyard, the community hall, and every stairwell within the entire complex. Kay was nowhere to be found. I had no choice but to call the police. A female police officer arrived about a half hour later, and Kay was still nowhere to be found. The officer checked the same areas we did with her flashlight and called her name. Still no Kay. The officer turned to me and started asking me questions. I pretty much told her my life story.

The officer looked at me and said, "Mom, this one is tough. I know you are doing what you can to make things better for your children, but you can't ignore the signs. Your daughter needs you and may be yearning for your attention. You have to find the balance."

Her words hit me in the chest like a ton of bricks. I broke down. I could never get a break. I was trying so hard, but I kept running into roadblocks everywhere I turned. I had taken one step forward and two steps back. I was always on a slope and could never get to the top. I did not know how to keep going. All I could picture was my little girl in a compromising situation that she could not get herself out of. I was at a loss for words. I acknowledged that I spent too many hours at work and I had to spend more time with my children. Once we exhausted the search for Kay, we walked back to the apartment.

As the officer was sharing some tips with me, Kay appeared. She saw the officer, her sister, and me, and had a nonchalant, don't-care attitude.

"Where were you?" I asked her.

"I went to a house party with some friends," she said. "I knew that if I asked you to go, you would have said no, so I decided to sneak out."

I was happy she was safe, but I was angry at her for the fear she placed in my heart. The officer asked to speak with her alone, and I went into the apartment. Before the officer left, she knocked on the door and told me to pay more attention to my children and who they were hanging around. She wished me good luck and left.

It was dawn when it was over, and I was exhausted. Kay had such a nasty attitude that if I had spoken to her at that time, I would have killed her. I told her we would talk about it later, and I went to my room and cried. Later that day, we had a long conversation, but I could tell that it was going through one ear and coming out the other. Her demeanor was one of defiance.

The next day, I went to the pool because I wanted to meet Angel. All the teenagers were there. Kay had been around her girlfriends for months and had not done anything like this, but now that there was this supposed boyfriend, there was a change in her behavior. In my heart, I believed that he had influenced her to leave her home in the middle of the night, and I needed to have a conversation with him. Shay pointed him out to me, and I called him over to talk.

I disliked him immediately. I went right into telling him I was disappointed that he would influence Kay to leave her home. I also told him Kay was too young to have a boyfriend, and I did not approve of their relationship. Angel was eighteen, tall and skinny with big, beautiful curls, and he was getting ready to graduate from high school. He listened to all that I had to say without interrupting. He was respectful, and his only responses were "Yes, ma'am" and "I am sorry, ma'am." I told him to leave my daughter alone. Somehow, I had a feeling it would not be the end of Angel.

One week later, Kay did it again. In all honesty, I was not as surprised as before because of how challenging she was the last time, even with the police officer. I had started to randomly check in on her when she went to sleep after that incident, but it was hard to do, especially being tired after a long day at work. I found myself falling asleep, then jumping up in the middle of the night in a cold sweat and rushing to her room to see if she was there. I loved my daughter—she was my life—but I felt as if she was in over her head with this group of friends. I had to face the truth that she was not willing to follow my rules even after the heartfelt conversations I had had with her. Whatever the officer had said to her in private the week prior was not enough to keep her at home.

Once I walked into Kay's room, I immediately noticed the doll's hair and the pillows that were covered up to look like her body. I knew what I needed to do to get it into her head that I was not playing. I put the lock on the window on the inside, so she would not be able to enter the house unless she came through the front door, to which I added a chain. That meant that she had to knock to get into the house. I went into her room, packed her clothes in a suitcase, and placed it by the front door.

I could not go to sleep, so I sat up all night waiting for her to return. I did not call the police this time and I did not go checking the stairwells of the apartment complex. I knew wherever she was, she was with Angel. In the early hours of the morning, I heard Kay trying to open her window to get in the apartment and it would not open. She had been gone for over five hours, and she had disrespected me and our home for the last time in this manner. She knocked on the window, and I heard but did not respond. Shay woke up and realized what was happening. After several attempts at the window, Kay walked to the front door and started knocking. I refused to let her in even though she was pleading for me to open the door. My heart was broken and tears were running down my face, but I felt that it was important for me to be firm with her. I waited for about thirty minutes until it was fully daylight. Finally, I opened the door but just enough to show her the packed suitcase and to tell her that I had bought an airline ticket to send her back to Jamaica to live with her father. I told her that I had asked Earl to take her to the airport. I closed the door without letting her in.

"You have no respect for me," I continued through the door. "And because you are a woman, you should go back to Jamaica and be the woman you want to be without having to play by the rules in my home."

Kay got the message this time. She started crying. Although my heart was hurting and I had lied about purchasing the airline ticket, I had to play tough to get through to my child. It took everything inside of me to not fold. She was at the door, knocking, crying, and begging me not to send her back to Jamaica.

"I'm sorry, Mommy, I am so sorry," she said. "I promise to never do it again. Please don't send me back to Jamaica."

Shay was crying and begging me to let her in. My heart could no longer take it, and I opened the door. I hugged my baby Kay and I cried with her. She never did it again. I knew she was in over her head and I had to get her away.

CHAPTER EIGHTEEN

HOPE RESTORED

Things were still going well at work. Over a span of two years, I was promoted twice, and the second position placed me in a senior role. I was the fine and fashion jewelry manager, and I also had responsibilities for fashion accessories. It was customary that the fine jewelry managers and the cosmetics managers were the senior managers in the stores because those departments were considered specialty and operated as a store within a store. I was recognized as Sales Manager of the Year and with that came great perks and benefits. I was also the manager in charge of employee recognition for the entire store. During corporate visits, I shined. My results were at the top in the store. I knew how to articulate about my business when I spoke to the buyers, planners, and regional executives. I was able to talk to the four-wall results, which were sales, shortage, operations, and employee relations. I had substantial growth over growth in all areas, both seasonally and yearly. I was also promoting staff members to next-level positions. I was rocking, and I felt confident.

Then one day, someone made a comment about the cheap clothes I wore to work. I felt embarrassed. Yes, I bought my clothes from Walmart and the casual department in the store, but I was always well put together. I had responsibilities that took precedent over expensive and brand-name apparel. My coworkers had no idea the hand I had been dealt in life. They had no clue I was a battered woman who sometimes still dealt with the effects of abuse. They didn't know that I cried every day when I was alone in my car because I felt lost. There was a hole in my heart. I still struggled with the fact that I had met a man who told me he would love me forever and then treated me like a doormat. They would never be able to tell that I had been homeless or evicted. I was hurt that some of my peers looked past my dedication and hard work and chose to laugh and talk about my cheap clothes behind my back.

In the mornings that followed, I found myself spending an inordinate amount of time trying to find something to wear that looked more expensive. It's unbelievable how one comment can erode everything you think about yourself. I was disappointed in myself that I allowed negative chatter to affect me in such a way. What I realized was that I was still severely emotionally damaged.

I became a little more reserved at work. Everything was getting to me. Just when I thought I was on a roll, I got depressed and overwhelmed. I felt empty and missed my mom more than ever. I would have been able to tell her what was said, what I was feeling, and she would have said a few words that would change everything for the better.

The overwhelm weighed me down. I started to feel very lethargic and not my usual energetic self. I scheduled an appointment to see my OBGYN, as I had not gone in years. During the examination, the doctor found that I had fibroids the size of golf balls. At the time, she counted seven. Due to the heavy bleeding, the fibroids were causing an iron deficiency, and with an iron deficiency comes a lack of energy. The doctor's recommendation was to do a laparoscopic myomectomy to remove the fibroids. She wanted it done immediately. I prayed for God to direct my path.

I took a few weeks off from work to have the procedure done. The surgery was a godsend. It took me away from the work environment for a while and allowed me to rest. Although I was healing, I did not realize how much I needed to relax my body and my mind. I slept and I started writing in my journal again, something that I had not done in a while. I was able to stay home and spend time with the girls, which was good for us. I truly believed that the effects of the emotional, psychological abuse and instability played a role in me having fibroids.

During my recovery, I found myself at a crossroads. It was the first time that I had a chance to sit and assess my life without interruption. I thought back to my journey coming to the United States as a naïve young lady, with the twists and turns, highs and lows, that got me to my current place. In every situation, no matter how bad, there was always a way out. Whether it was through my daughters, a stranger, a friend, or a situation that presented itself, there was always a ram in the bush. It finally dawned on me that God had been with me all along. He had provided the escapes, the ways out, the silver linings in the cloudy days, the rainbows when it rained. He never left me, and when I almost took my life, He used the gift of my child to save me. Then He gave my other child the wisdom to help us escape.

I got on my knees and broke down. I thanked God for keeping me, for saving me, for protecting me, for never leaving me, for blessing me, and for giving me grace. Alone in my room, I cried out to Him, and for the first time in what seemed like forever, I felt His presence wrapping me in a warm embrace and comforting me. I felt a peace in my heart that I had never known. I had some answers to the questions on that left page in my journal, and I needed to write my dreams and goals on paper.

At the crossroads were two signs: left and right. I needed to make a choice of which way to travel. The left held all the painful memories, setbacks, and adversities of my past. I would point the finger at everything and everyone but me. I could say I had the right intentions, but someone forced me to make the wrong decisions. I could play the blame game and say woe is me for all that I had endured. Or I could go right. Traveling right meant acknowledging my mistakes, accepting that I was accountable, forgiving myself, and learning to love the woman I was. I chose right!

I started going to church and truly seeking a relationship with the Heavenly Father. That was the thing that had been missing from my life. I knew it would not be roses and sunshine all the time, but it was the start of a different journey. It had to be an intentional process.

***

When I went back to work, I felt like a new person. I walked in with my head held high, in my cheap clothes, and never gave the negative chatter another thought. I was adamant that I would be known for my integrity and excellent work ethic. That was all that mattered.

A few weeks later, I got a call at work and was offered an opportunity to interview for a position in a department store in the Washington, DC, market. I was flabbergasted. I had only been to Washington, DC, once with Earl, but from what I remembered, I loved it. The company flew me up, reserved a hotel for me, and sent a car to pick me up for the interview. It was great. They offered me a higher position and a lot more money than the job I currently held, so I put in my two weeks notice at work. This was the ultimate light at the end of a very dark tunnel. It was my chance to get out of Florida and take my kids to a new environment.

I had a family meeting to ask Kay and Shay how they felt about moving. Shay was super excited. When

I asked Kay how she felt, her answer melted me and brought tears to my eyes.

"Mom, let's go," she said. "I need a new start. I am in over my head and I want to start over in a new place."

That was the green light I needed.

We knew no one in Washington, DC, but we had each other. After all we had been through, I knew we could survive anything. The company I worked for denied my notice and refused to let me go work for another department store. They countered the offer to keep me, but I turned it down. When they asked me why, I told them it was important that I left Florida to pursue a new start for the sake of my children. They went back to the drawing board and added an additional $5,000 to beat the other company's offer with a huge promotion to human resources in the Washington, DC, market. I thought my heart was going to stop. We are talking about a primarily Monday to Friday, nine-to-five job in retail as a human resources coordinator. To top it off, they offered me an additional $5,000 in cash for out-of-pocket expenses, a moving company to pack and store our furniture, and corporate housing for eight weeks in Arlington, Virginia. Oh my god, I had hit the jackpot! I did not see that coming. I accepted without hesitation and I called the other company to withdraw my acceptance. This was the break I needed, and God had showed up for me.

I went to visit my mom's grave and told her I was leaving. I knew in my heart she was happy for me. I promised to come back and visit. I also called Earl to say goodbye. He had been a constant in our lives, always checking in on us to make sure we were doing well. He was sad to see us go but happy that we were moving in the right direction with our lives. I was ready for the change. We needed healing and restoration, and Kay would not have to sink in the environment that was swallowing her up.

On July 3, the moving truck came. We packed our car and drove to Orlando, Florida. We drove the car onto the auto-train platform and settled into our seats for the ride to Northern Virginia. We could not contain our excitement. The train ride was soothing. We were scheduled to arrive in DC the next day, July 4, to check into our corporate home.

I was so happy that I laid my head back and fell asleep.

***

I woke up in the desert with sand all around me. I was looking for Kay, but she was nowhere in sight. I started calling out her name, only to notice that I was being chased. I started running but suddenly felt a sharp pain in my right heel. I screamed. I looked down to see a large piece of broken glass lodged in my heal, which was bleeding profusely. I was running but limping on my right toes. Whoever was chasing me was gaining momentum, and I still could not find my daughter. I noticed there were people in front of me running as well, and I called out to them to help me. They could not hear what I was saying, and they kept running. I had a large bag over my shoulder, and in order to keep going, I dropped the bag and left it in the sand. I was weeping because I knew I was leaving my daughter behind me, but I was scared of the people who were in pursuit of me. The pain in my heel was excruciating, and I knew they would get me anytime now. How could I lose them so I could go back and search for my daughter? What type of mother would not look for her baby? If she is lost in this desert, I know she will be crying, calling my name, and looking for me. Oh, God, please help me, I cried, as the Federales pulled their guns on me and said, "Freeze." I turned around to face them, fear gripping me, and I jumped out of my sleep.

I looked around and saw that I was still sitting on the train car, and my girls were sleeping across from me. I was sweating, and my heart was pounding. Was this a nightmare or was it a reality? I looked out the window, and the memories, although somewhat broken, started coming back. What happened that caused me to leave my bags in the desert?

REFLECTIONS

In writing this book, I asked my step-daughter, Damika (Dami), and my daughter Kay to write from their hearts what they recalled from their childhoods. Here are their words, unedited as they sent it to me.

From Dami

January 5, 2016, 11:09 p.m.

I was hesitant because I wasn't sure that what I remembered was something you could use for your book. So I guess I'll just start at the beginning. You can decide.

I was 11 years old when you moved in with us. My father's girlfriend Diane and her daughter had just moved out. I left for the weekend, and when I came back, you were there. I was a little unhappy. Quite literally just a couple days before, another woman was living with us. Diane was the only adult figure I had in my life at that time and you can imagine she took care of me most of the time since my dad ran the streets so much. I just remembered that you were young (Diane was 38 I believe) and you called me "Dami" and I just thought it was strange. You made me hotdogs on white bread for lunch, and I remembered being afraid the other kids would see it. You won me over when you made the chicken seasoned with some type of ketchup sauce. I called it ketchup chicken and it was really good.

You were right when you said if things weren't written down it will be hard to remember. I remember a lot, but there is a whole lot more I don't remember. But I don't remember why, why did he do the things that he did to you? I don't remember seeing him hit you, I just remember hearing it. My heart would drop and it was a horrible dreadful feeling. You knew something bad was happening to someone and you couldn't do anything about it. I always knew my dad was mean but this was the first time it was evident by the way he treated you.

I guess when I was around 12 I spent most of the time at Sybil's house and I came home on weekends. We talked a lot I guess because there was no one else. I remember you telling me about a miscarriage and I wondered if he had beat you did that make you lose the baby. I remember when you left the first time and went to visit your sisters in Florida. I missed you but I didn't want you to come back because even though I was young I knew the way he treated you was just so wrong. I remember overhearing him tell you how sick he was and that you should come back but he was just downstairs.

Remember the gate that he used to lock you in the house? You had no key to be able to get out of the house. If I came home from school we would have to wait for him to come and unlock the door. I remember we broke the lock on the back gate. I even remember having to go buy diapers for Shayana and squeezing it between the bars on the front gate. I don't quite remember but I'm guessing I had to climb over the back gate to get back in. I'm not sure. For some reason I remember us laughing so I'm wondering if that's really what I had to do.

When you were pregnant with Shay, you had two maternity dresses, do you remember that? He always took care of himself but that's about it.

Do you remember Lolita? We found his cell phone bill and there was a number he called repeatedly. We called the number and got a female's voicemail. He was in DC and Lee called the house to say something. We called the number back and the female answered saying she just came back from DC with my father. I don't remember what became of that.

Remember your try at becoming a smoker? You would buy Virginia Slims, lol.

Remember you told me about the females that jumped out of the car because they thought my dad was hitting you. I believed he was but you lied and said that he wasn't.

And I remembered Richard and at one point he was like the only friend you had. I think I got a little jealous because it was just the two of us in the house and I guess I was jealous of the friendship. There was an incident in Jersey. I guess you two still had phone conversations. I don't know if he called the number back or something but I know at the end of the day it was believed that I was the one calling Richard. No one likes to take the blame for anything but I was old enough to understand that it was better for him to think it was me and not you.

The neighbor Kelly next door told me that once when she was hanging out with her friends in Camden, my father and his friends were hitting on her and her friends. She told him who she was and he begged her not to tell me. She told me right before I ran away and it was still embarrassing.

There was a lot that happened and I really wish that I remembered more details. Forgive me if some of the grammar is a bit off, I'm using the speech app on the iPad.

I do thank you for being one of the very few adults to provide me with love and stability when both of my parents had totally failed me. I know it sounds silly to say but there is still a part of me that wishes that I could have helped you.

I visited my father in the hospital a couple of months ago. For a moment he seemed really sincere and told me that he really regretted the person he was and he wished he had been a better father. About five minutes later he took it back. He said he didn't regret anything that he had done. I asked him "nothing?" He said "nothing." I said Joan didn't deserve the way you treated her.

He said she wasn't an angel. I said maybe not an angel but she certainly did nothing to deserve the way you treated her. He had no choice but to agree.

I wish I remembered more details, and that's what took me so long. I just wish I had remembered more. I hope this helps.

Damika

***

From Kay

January 5, 2016, 4:01 p.m.

I've always had this ability to read people. From the moment I met someone I would get an instant impression that would let me know if they were "good people." It was the same the first time I met my stepfather. I was about 7 years old and the moment I met him I knew. Kids are pure, innocent. I think they can see that innocence in others. Just as they can see the good, they can see the bad. That's what I saw and felt the first time I met him. He looked at me and I looked at him and in that moment, he knew that I knew what he really was, and I think that's the second he decided he wasn't going to like me.

During my stay in New Jersey there were a lot of instances of abuse I remember witnessing and experiencing. I saw my mother screamed at and belittled. I saw her beaten till bloody on the bathroom floor with my sister and I both standing at the doorway. I remember being in the car to go pick up my mother from work and knowing she'd been waiting outside for my stepdad for hours. I remember my stepsister running away shortly after I moved in. She was kind and sad and in her own way I think she was trying to warn me. I believe a part of that sadness was the fact she knew she was leaving and wished she could help me because she knew that I had no idea the things I was about to face.

I spent most of my days alone. After school I would come home to an empty house. My stepdad would be out doing whatever it is he did and my sister would be with him, while my mom was at work. Those days were the worst. I didn't know it then but I was too young to be left home alone for hours, so for that reason my stepdad ordered that I was never to go outside or near the window. I wasn't allowed to watch television in case the noise may alert a neighbor that someone was home. For that same reason when it got dark I couldn't turn on the lights.

I remember always being hungry. I wasn't allowed to touch the food in the pantry or the fridge. Mostly I remember feeling lonely all the time. I used to just try and make myself small and invisible to him because I really believed he hated me.

He never beat me. He punished me in other ways. He isolated me. He kept me from being able to have a relationship with my little sister least I somehow corrupt her. Anything that he could blame on me he would. A scratch on the floor, a spot on the carpet, mark on the wall, any mess that was made by my little sister was somehow my doing, so I was punished.

There was no happiness in that house. My mother and sister and I tried very hard to make our own though. There were no birthdays or Christmas. So we would celebrate in secret. Decorate, celebrate and take it all down before he came home. We would even order pizza and eat it in bed! And every night without fail, my sister and I would sit in bed with mom and read Psalm 91. Till this day I can recite the entire thing.

Abuse does different things to different people. During my time with my stepdad I could have let him break me. But I didn't. Instead in my own way I fought back. When he would leave me home alone and locked out of every room, I learned to pick a lock. I wasn't allowed to watch television so I took an old one that wasn't working anyway and learned to rig and wire it. From then on I took my punishments in stride. I learned how to be unemotional and a problem solver. It made me stronger. Seeing my mother beaten down and defeated gave me focus. I was determined to convince her to leave. And I did. But the abuse also had more far reaching effects. It shaped my actions and personality in such a way that my relationship with my mother was never how it could have been.

All I ever wanted to do was protect her. So in the spirit of that, things that happened to me in New Jersey I kept mostly to myself. With everything she had to endure on a daily basis, the abuse, my sisters medical problems, feeling like she was isolated from her family members, the fear, all the stress at work. I just didn't want to add to any of it.

So I grew up never wanting to add to her stress. I wanted to keep my pain away from her. What I didn't realize at the time was that in doing so I would end up keeping not just my feelings or pain from her, but an actual part of me. My intent was to shield her; instead I inadvertently created this distance between us, this barrier that we never quite bridged.

That is how abuse affected me. I felt like my stepfather took my mother from me, both in a literal and emotional sense. Literal in the way that he charmed her into leaving Jamaica at which time I could not go with her so I had to stay behind. And emotional because I had to suppress and make light of the things I endured in hopes of protecting her. And the only way I knew how to do that was by pushing her away.

I don't think she every really figured out where it came from, this distance between us. I know over the years she thought it was because I was angry with her for things that have happened to me. Possibly some childhood or teenage angst that I'm still holding onto, or maybe she's just chalked it up to the paradigm that is the mother-daughter relationship. The truth is it's because I still keep a small part of me at a distance. Hidden. I'm still trying to shield her from anything that might make her feel bad or guilty because none of it was her fault. I love my mother dearly and I don't ever want my hurt to hurt her.

She used to say that I was her strength and the thing is, I still am and always will be.

The things I've experienced will always be a part of who I am, but I don't dwell on them. I'm whole, happy and healed. I'm grateful for my life and my family and feel incredibly blessed.

Kay

RESOURCES

If you know someone that may be in an abusive situation, instead of asking why don't you just leave, offer your help and ask instead, "How can I help you?" or "What can I do to assist you?" Feel free to reference chapter nine in this book for ideas that you or someone could use.

"*Why doesn't she just leave?* It's the question many people ask when they learn that a woman is suffering battery and abuse. But if you are in an abusive relationship, you know that it's not that simple. Ending a significant relationship is never easy. It's even harder when you've been isolated from your family and friends, psychologically beaten down, financially controlled, and physically threatened," Source: *Breaking the Silence Handbook*

If you are being abused, remember:

- You are not to blame for being battered or mistreated.

- You are not the cause of your partner's abusive behavior.

- You deserve to be treated with respect.

- You deserve a safe and happy life.

- Your children deserve a safe and happy life.

- Don't stay for the kids; leave for the kids.
- You are not alone. There are people waiting to help.
- Find someone you trust and confide in them

There are many resources available for abused and battered women, including crisis hotlines, shelters—even job training, legal services, and childcare. Start by reaching out today.

If you're in an abusive relationship and fear for your life, call 911.

If you need assistance or to find the nearest shelter, call the National Domestic Violence Hotline at 1-800-799-SAFE or 1-800-799-7233. Or online chat is available 24 hours a day, 7 days a week, 365 days a year.

To get more information, resources or tips on how you can create an exit strategy, go to the website for the National Coalition Against Domestic Violence, NCADV.org.

To volunteer or to become an advocate, go to futureswithoutviolence.org.

Here is a list of Facebook support groups:

- End Violence Against Women
- Domestic Violence Awareness and Support
- Domestic Violence Support for Women
- Domestic Violence Victim Support Group

ABOUT THE AUTHOR

Joan T. Randall is a certified speaker and coach whose mission is to impact lives to change the outcomes. A survivor of domestic abuse, she has committed her life to help victims become victors and take back their power. She is a certified domestic violence victim's advocate and volunteers for Safe Alliance Domestic Violence Shelter for Women and Kids. For her work, she was honored with the Philanthropic Award for Community Leadership in 2017, and the Women's Leadership Award in 2016.

An award-winning, bestselling author, Joan has published *90 Days to a Victorious You*, *Finding a Path to Victory*, and *Loving Me from A to Z*. In her spare time, she enjoys dancing, listening to music, and writing. She currently lives in Concord, North Carolina, with her husband, Bill Randall, and is the proud mother of three daughters: Kaydene Caban, Shay Oakley, and Brianna Randall and her only son: Brandon Randall.

To connect, visit joantrandall.com

CPSIA information can be obtained
at www.ICGtesting.com
Printed in the USA
FSHW021453110520
70130FS